POST, LIKE, RETWEET

THE TRUTH ABOUT SOCIAL MEDIA

**WHEELING JESUIT UNIVERSITY
COPYEDITING CLASS 2012**

ISBN: 1477428305
ISBN 13: 9781477428306

Library of Congress Control Number: 2012908624
CreateSpace Independent Publishing Platform,
North Charleston, SC

INTRODUCTION

TYLER GLOVER

According to Quora.com, there are nearly 300 million tweets sent per day this year, over 500 million Facebook users, and 48% of those users between the age of 18 and 34 check their Facebook as soon as they wake up. Every aspect of our lives has been affected by constant status updates, watching videos, and obsessively checking our smart phones. Daily routines will never be the same. For example, a normal morning ritual used to consist of waking up, taking a shower, telling your family "good morning," eating breakfast, and heading to work or school. Now, the process takes twice as long because we wake up, check our Facebook updates, tweet "good morning twitter fam," maybe watch a YouTube video or two, then finally make it out of bed to start our day.

So, what exactly is social media? According to the Merriam-Webster dictionary, social media is defined as: "forms of electronic communication ([such] as Web sites for social networking and microblogging) through which users create online communities to share information, ideas, personal messages, and other content ([such] as videos). This is not to be confused with social networking, which is a part of social media that focuses on keeping groups of like-minded people together in a site that facilitates communication." Social media covers a much broader spectrum than social networking, so by addressing social media, we are covering social networking, along with all the other aspects of electronic communication.

Some common examples of these forms of electronic communication are sites that we hear about and use every day such as Facebook, Twitter, and MySpace. There are also up and coming sites such as Pinterest, dating sites such as E-Harmony, and even the video sharing giant YouTube is considered a social media site. As you can see from this small list, many different websites are covered under the broad category of social media, so clearly there is a multitude of information that needs to be shared on this topic and about these particular sites. It is nearly impossible to put an actual number on how many social media sites are out there because they seemingly pop up overnight. It is also impossible for us to cover all those sites, so our intention is to cover social media as a whole, and to also focus on some of the more popular sites, as well as touching on some new, growing sites. This will enable us to provide you with as much information as possible, while still keeping the book readable and not turning it into a giant, complicated encyclopedia.

As a class, we decided to write a book about social media because although many people use it, nobody knows absolutely everything about it. We felt like this topic needed addressed because every day we see someone using social media incorrectly or hear horror stories of mishaps online. For example, my mother is extremely awkward on Facebook. If she comments on my wall she types "Love, Mom," after it every time. I always tell her "Mom; it tells me who posted it there, you don't have to type who you are." But, she continues to do the same thing every single time. There is also the story of the "Craig's List Killer" in which a person used social media in order to trick people into showing up for a "job" only to kill them on their arrival. I am not stating that we can prevent murders or make moms less awkward necessarily, but we are providing the information here to raise awareness of potential scams, show internet etiquette, and have a basic understanding of how social media works.

Our generation has grown up with social media. So while no one person can know everything about a topic as broad as social media, our combined knowledge should be extremely helpful to other generations. As we developed, so did social media sites. We used Friendster and MSN messenger back when they were by far the cool thing to do. We then went MySpace crazy for years, obsessing over our "top friends" and designing our own page. Then Facebook came along and we all jumped over to that bandwagon because, well, everyone else was. Now, we are constant tweeters. So what if no one even cares about what our little hundred and forty character messages have to say? We'll still tweet it, and then tweet about nobody reading our tweets! Undoubtedly, a newer, better social media site will attract our attention next, and the pattern will continue. Our generation is tech savvy, constantly on a phone or computer, and our social lives are completely different than previous generations. We couldn't survive without the internet because we rely on it to help develop relationships, answer questions that we are unsure of, and we would really struggle to write a paper without it. We aren't doctors or professors, we aren't even professional writers. What we are is generation Y, and we feel that we have knowledge about social media that we need to share with other generations.

Social Media has really only been around since the 1990's, and it has already impacted the way we behave every day. From the popularity of Facebook to the rise of smart phones, it is nearly impossible to avoid social media. Every commercial on television refers to their Facebook or Twitter page to help businesses stay connected to customers, every celebrity tweets multiple times a day so they can stay in the spotlight, and everyone's grandma now has a Facebook page. Social media is unavoidable, and a book needed to be written to describe what should and should not be done on those sites, to help explain confusing topics about social media, and to provide information that many people may have never even thought about.

This book is meant to provide answers to mothers who are seeking advice on how to keep their children safe online, first time social media users who really need help getting started, or even someone who uses social media daily and may not be taking full advantage of its features. In a society that is increasingly reliant on social media, this book was necessary to develop in order to provide solid foundations for anyone seeking to use these sites. From someone who doesn't know what a tweet is, to a person with a thousand Facebook friends, there is something to be learned by reading this book. Social media has changed the world, so we believe the world should be as knowledgeable about social media as possible. Generation Y grew up with social media, so we are the perfect choice to educate all other generations on what you should, and shouldn't do online.

CHAPTER 1

Colin Lawler – "Full Speed Ahead'

1. What does "LOL" mean?

    a)   Lots of Love
    b)   Licks of lollypops
    c)   Laugh out Loud

2. What is the difference between an Inbox Message and a Chat Message?

3. What is a Hashtag (#)?

For those of you picking up this book and wondering what exactly it is you will be reading about, allow me to explain. What you have in front of you is essentially your own guide to understanding the generational phenomena that has come to be known as social media. Now you may not believe that this technological giant has taken hold of humanity's existence, but it truly has. The speed at which people demand information has grown exponentially through centuries, and today the demand is even greater. As a result of this "need for speed," social media sites such as Facebook, Twitter, MySpace, etc... have developed a unique "language" of their own. However, first a brief history lesson is in order.

Communication was not always as easy as it is today. It was not until approximately 900 B.C.E. that a postal service was even developed (we have the Chinese to thank for that)[1]. Writing was a rarity and information was generally passed along via word of mouth. However, as time marched on, people demanded information to be readily available. The eldest form of writing dates back to 1400 B.C.E. from China in the east. In the west, the Greeks developed an alphabet allowing speech to be represented by symbols. Thus, writing was born. Between 200 B.C.E. and 100 B.C.E., messengers on horseback would collect written information and relay the messages back and forth between station points that had been established (sound familiar?)[2]. By 14 C.E., in the process of the rule of the Roman Empire, Roman officials had established a postal service, connecting the all relay points back to the hub of the empire: Rome.[3]

Keep in mind that the postal services of the ancient world were not what they are today. Initially, the postal service, especially in Rome, was created solely for government use. Time was the deciding factor in allowing postage to be a commercial commodity. Commercializing the postal service was the first groundbreaking step for the information-sharing industry. Before the sending and receiving of letters, individuals had no other choice than to travel to a neighboring town where a relative may have lived in order to "hear" from them. Sometimes those "neighboring" towns were either a great distance away or not so neighborly. The time in which delivery took was infinitely greater because of technological constraints. The distance between the city of Wheeling, WV and Philadelphia, PA is roughly 360 miles and is about a six-hour car ride[4]. Back in ancient times, traveling to Philly from Wheeling would have transpired by walking or riding a horse through harsh terrain as direct roads had not been developed. All of the stories of people disappearing during their travels? Yeah, they came from delivering letters. What the postal service did was place all of the danger of mail delivery on one person's head.

Between 1450 C.E. and 1455 C.E., commercialization of communication boomed[5]. Newspapers began appearing in European cities providing, for those who bought them, information concerning what was happening in the world. By 1455, the speed at which these papers were produced accelerated with Johannes Gutenberg's invention of a printing press with moveable metal type.[6] Thousands of papers could be created in a few hours. The expectation had been set; news was what was happening, not what happened.

Moving quickly through the centuries to the opening of the American west gives a perspective far more relatable to home. In 1861, the United States started the Pony Express with the sole purpose of improving communication between the settling, uncivilized west and the already settled, technologically established east[7]. At this point in time, the fastest way to travel was by horse and so messages could always be delayed or arrive several days, weeks or months behind schedule. Effort was put forth in writing letters to peoples farther away because of how long it took for mail to be delivered. In the times of the great westward expansion, letters were multiple pages and outlined several situations and attitudes peoples of the plains were experiencing. Generally speaking, complaints about the system did not exist for two reasons. The first was due to the technology of the time. The second, those living during that time period did not know any better.

Radio and television's establishment worked more for the commercial masses in form of both receiving information and entertainment. The important distinction to realize, however is that both radio and television did not serve a personal purpose. Commercial radio reported the news and other entertainment blocks. If Mrs. Johnson, living in Cleveland, wished to check on her son in Albuquerque, NM she would not be able to do it through the channels of commercial radio or television through that matter. Communication in these mediums was (and still are for the most part) directed one way. Eventually information seeking became much more personalized.

Defying traditional means of communication at the time, Alexander Graham Bell invented the telephone in 1876[8]. Suddenly, could travel through a receiver powered by electricity and shot out another end. The closest medium that had existed prior to this moment was Samuel Morse's code for the electric telegraph. Morse code was not a conventional conversation however because the "clicks" and "spaces" needed to be interpreted into words. Bell's telephone allowed people to talk with other people directly (but indirectly) over the perplexities of their lives.

A century and a couple decades later the cell phone would once again revolutionize communications and set a stage for the foundations of social media language.

As time pressed forward, improvement were made to each of the communication mediums that have already been discussed. Both electricity and the industrial revolution transformed the printing press from a hand-cranked press to a working of mechanical presses and conveyer belts able to generate thousands of newspapers in minutes rather than hours. Postage could be delivered in days through the use of automobiles and airplanes. Cell phones freed everyday travelers from being confined to wires, allowing movement.

Each advancement brought the demand for better, faster, and stronger communication. The computer's creation in the late 1970's was only outdone by the release of the "world wide web" for public use[9]. Internet capability, in the famous words of AOL, made "fast faster." Even today, the Internet is still the main source for retrieval of information. Much of that information is exchanged through communication sites designed to connect people together for the purpose of networking i.e. social media.

Now that the general history lesson is over, it is imperative that the language of social media be put into terms so that you the reader possess a better understanding of this remerging and constantly evolving communication tool.

Text messaging for the cell phone set the foundation of the social media language (SML). SML can be generalized as a series of abbreviations of regular says, phrases or stand-ins of words. Almost all of these abbreviations are comprised of letters representing a corresponding word. For example, a common phrase used in social messaging is "lol" and each letter stands for a word. The phrase "lol" stands for the larger phrase "laugh out loud." The formula for placing together a social media word is simple: take the first letter of each of the words you want to type and have those letters form the word. Keep in mind that not all phrases can be translated into social media language. For example, translating the phrase "what are you doing" would not come to "wayd." Instead the phrase could be read one of two ways: "what r u doin" or "wat r u doin." Common phrases are only translated to the three-letter system. In other cases discretion should be advised when abbreviating words.

The reason why SML (you have permission to call it slang language as well because at its core, it is) has been adopted by so many relates back to why people demanded improvements in communication. The movie *Talladega Nights* says it best, "America is all about speed…"[10] Speed is the driving force behind SML. It is faster to type three letters than it is to type three words. The concern is on the messages speed even if it is only barely legible. If writing this way bothers you, there is good news. Facebook and other social media sites have shifted from in their use of language. The default abbreviations still exist ("lol" for example) and are used, but more and more people are using appropriate English in their postings (if you are unfamiliar with that word it will be explained in the next paragraph).

Some social media sites utilize words they have coined or created, which are specific to the given site. For example, a statement written by an individual to his or her own Facebook or another person is called a post. Similarly, Twitter utilizes similar language with the information posted to its pages. Twitter also uses symbols to communicate information. An example of this is @. This symbol is used to specifically target a person or persons in a tweet. A list of these associated symbols as well as their use and definition are available in the glossary section following the end of the chapter.

At the moment, hundreds of social media sites exist on the Internet, each a variation of another in some shape or form. The top 15 sites are:

1. Facebook
2. Twitter
3. LinkedIn
4. MySpace
5. Google plus
6. DevianArt
7. LiveJournal
8. Tagged
9. Orkut
10. CafeMom
11. Ning
12. Meetup
13. myLife
14. myYearbook
15. Badoo

Social media is a constantly evolving entity. You will learn a brief history of that evolution in the next chapter.

REFERENCES

1. "Chronological and Thematic Studies on the History of Information and Media," Jeremy Norman, accessed February 12, 2012, http://www.historyofinformation.com/index.php?category=Communication

2. IBib "Information and Media"

3. IBib "Information and Media"

4. IBib "Information and Media"

5. "History of Communication," last modified March 11, 1998, http://inventors.about.com/library/inventors/bl_history_of_communication.htm

6. IBib "History"

7. IBib "History"

8. "Communication Technologies and World History," last modified December 31, 2005, http://www.worldhistorysite.com/communication.html

9. IBib "History"

10. IBib "Communication"

CHAPTER 2

Jenn Elias– "Evolution of Social Media"

1. What was the first type of Social networking site?

2. When was Facebook founded?

3. What percent of young people use social media sites?

Evolution of Social Media

When computers were invented, no one knew what was really being created. Newly developed technology allowed for new ways of communication. The invention of social media and networking websites replaced traditional handwritten letters and telephone calls. Today, over two billion people are connected to the internet one way or another[1], and an average of 90 percent of young people are participating in social networking cites daily [2].

We live in a fast-paced world. When the internet and e-mail were first created, the rapid response of an e-mail was not fast enough. How did you know if the person you sent an e-mail to was online at the moment or not? Therefore, America Online (AOL), created instant messaging (better known as AIM) in 1995. According to AIM's website, AIM is "a communication tool. It allows you to keep in touch with many people through text, video, and multimedia chat. [3]" Through instant messaging, an internet user has the ability to maintain a list of people either of their friends or with whom they wanted to interact. The list was often referred to this as the "buddy list." It allowed you to have all your contacts in one place and be able to see who was and who was not online at any given moment. From here, the internet user is able to instantly message any person on their list who was listed as being online. Other statuses available included being offline, away, or invisible (online without others online being able to tell). When officially released in March of 1996, it was only available to AOL subscribers until it was launched world-wide in May of 1997. At one time, AOL was the largest instant messaging market in North America. It not only included the buddy list and person-to-person instant messaging, but also had chat rooms, the ability to share files, web links, streaming content and personalization features. To personalize one's AIM, an internet user created a unique screen name including either his or her name, initials, favorite sport or television show, or any unique combination of numbers and letters. In addition, icons and buddy info provided those who saw your screen name with additional information about yourself. Through AOL's instant messaging system, internet users and the world were able to have instant communication between people [4].

Internet users now had a way of interacting with one another through AOL's creation; however, Jonathan Abrams had a different idea that expanded upon AOL's instant messaging technology. In 2002, Abrams founded an online social networking service called Friendster. It is "one of the oldest and first of the popular social networking sites boom". Through this social media website, individuals virtually connected to others through communities. Circles were displayed showing individual friends' profile pictures. Each circle has a line drawn (similar to a web) connecting them to another contact on your friend list. Friendster connects you with other "like-minded people" to share information and networks. Through Friendster, users could find old friends, new friends, classmates, co-workers, etc., by posting blogs, messages, discussions, e-mails, and interacting with friends. With over 50 million users worldwide, Friendster was an excellent website to make meaningful connections; yet, today, due to the rise of other more popular social networking websites, Friendster has become a social gaming website [2].

Chris DeWolf and Tom Anderson, member of Friendster.com, recognized the potential of social networking websites, and in 2003, they launched a similar yet more developed social networking website called MySpace.com. At release, the website was intended for actors, musicians, and artists. Local bands and agents created profiles on the website as a marketing tool. However, eight months after its creation, MySpace quickly expanded to become available for all internet users.

MySpace focused on "self-expression tapping into what young people were passionate about: expressing themselves, interacting with friends, and consuming popular culture." The website itself let users control their own pages and posts. Each page or profile was blank until the owner did whatever he wanted with it, essentially creating his own space or their "MySpace." Users' pages featured their pictures, friends, and posts. It was a place where users could interact not only with their friends, but with the world as well. According to an article by Jason Illian, MySpace is "not just a social networking site, but also a media hosting site that is part chat room, part movie theater, part shopping mall, part bar, and part concert that is open 24 hours a day, 7 days a week, 365 days a year." [5]

After two years, the number of MySpace user profiles quickly jumped from two million to eighty million. MySpace continued to grow and did not see a significant decrease until 2008, four years after yet another social networking website named Facebook was invented. MySpace allowed users to "search their own channels and go where they want[ed] to go and, in doing so, it continue[d] to push technology into new and exciting territories." [5] Today, according to its website, Myspace is "a leading social entertainment destination powered by the passions of fans...by providing a highly personalized experience around entertainment and connecting people to the music, celebrities, TV, movies, and games that they love." [6]

In 2005, a different type of social media website was created that allowed for the sharing and uploading of videos. This website was known as Youtube.com. YouTube was founded by three men: Chad Hurley, Steve Chen, and Jawed Karim, after the three of them worked together at PayPal as engineers and designers. The idea of YouTube came about after they experienced difficulty in trying to share videos with each other. Chen immediately recognized the idea and brought it to the market. On April 23, the first video, "Me at the Zoo", was uploaded. By December, YouTube was visited over 50 million times a day. The website quickly became popular as people began putting YouTube links on their MySpace pages. By May of 2006, YouTube became the "tenth most visited site in the United States." [7]

Harvard student Mark Zuckerberg and his friend Eduardo Saverin created yet another social networking website, similar to MySpace, known as Facebook. Originally named Facemash, the website compared photos of two students asking users which student was hotter. After this site was shutdown, Zuckerberg began writing a new website code and in February of 2004, thefacebook was created. Originally spread only throughout the dorms of Harvard's campus, thefacebook was well received and soon extended to Stanford and Yale University[8].

In August of 2005, Zuckerberg dropped out of college and dropped the "the" to newly named Facebook. At the time, Facebook's users consisted strictly of college students who had to sign up via assigned school or institution email addressed. In 2005, "approximately 85% of the students in the supported colleges [had] a Facebook account, with 60% of them logging in daily." By 2006, Facebook had recognized over thirty thousand schools, college, universities, and organizations to access their website. By September of 2005, Facebook was available to high school students in addition to the already college crowd, and, in 2006, Facebook opened to anyone over the age of thirteen with a valid e-mail address[9].

Facebook has become what it is today through its use of the profile page. A typical Facebook profile consists of a person's information, including anything from educational backgrounds, religious views, favorite movies, music, and television shows, relationship status, sex, birthdate, address, and email as well as status updates, friends, photos, notes, groups, and most importantly, the wall. The wall of Facebook page is where friends of the user can post anything from words, photos, links, and more. It also contains the basic information of the Facebook user. A Facebook user decides through privacy settings who can see their page. A page can be set to be viewable by all users or only those who are one's "friends," just like other social networking websites allow. In addition to these features, Facebook also allows for private messaging between friends where only those involved in the conversation can see what is communicated. Groups, events, birthday reminders, games, applications, and pages are also included on the Facebook website [10]. Facebook has grown to more than 800 million active users, yet Twitter has become the new budding social media networking phenomena [11]. Twitter was created by Jack Dorsey in March of 2006, wanting to "have a dispatch service that connects us on our phones using text." When launched, the original product name of "twttr" was used until the creators acquired what is now to be known as Twitter.com. When created, Twitter had users sending their messages via text messages to a "40404" number. Messages longer than 160 characters were typically split between text messages. To solve this problem, the creators, known as the "Twitter Team," decided to limit the messages to 140 characters to leave room for the username in front. Twitter became a place where users could express their thoughts, whereabouts, ideas, quotes, or other information in 140 characters or less through statuses known as "tweets" that are posted to the Twitter website. Twitter users can personalize their profiles by uploading a picture, changing their pages' background design, and giving a brief description (140 characters or less) about themselves. Users' friends are known as "followers" in that their tweets show up in their timelines when they access Twitter. Twitter is not only used by everyday people but also celebrities, news stations, sports teams, and more. Who would have believed Twitter creator Jack Dorsey when he tweeted, "One could change the world with one hundred and forty characters"? [12]

Today, social media is at our fingertips. At any moment, we can log into our social media sites and be updated instantly. With the development of cell phones and their mobile applications, we can access MySpace, Facebook, Twitter, LinkedIn, YouTube, and all the other social media networking sites at any given moment. Mobile phones even provide users an option to receive pop-up notifications any time an action on one of the social media applications occurs. Through social media and our instant access, we are connecting to the world at every instance.

REFERENCES

1. 20 Stunning Social Media Statistics Plus Infographic, Jeff Bullas, last modified September, 2011. http://www.jeffbullas.com

2. The History of Friendster, WebUpon, last modified April 1, 2008. http://webupon.com/social-networks

3. AIM FAQ, AIM, last modified 2012. http://www.aim.com/faq

4. How Instant Messaging Works, How Stuff Works, last modified 2004. http://vclass.mgt.psu.ac.th/~parinya/MISMBA2004/sectionII/hardware-howstuffworks/HSW-communication/instant-messaging.pdf

5. A Place for Friends, Random History, last modified August 14, 2008. http://www.randomhistory.com/2008/08/14_myspace.html

6. About Us, MySpace, last modified 2012. http://www.myspace.com/Help/AboutUs?pm_cmp=ed_footer

7. History of YouTube, Article Alley, last modified March 31, 2010. http://artlaco.articlealley.com/history-of-youtube-1482289.html

8. Facebook – The Complete Biography, Mashable Social Media, last modified August 25, 2006. http://mashable.com/2006/08/25/facebook-profile/

9. Facebook Notes, Facebook, last modified April 26, 2011. www.facebook.com

10. Facebook Profile, Facebook, last modified April 26, 2011. www.facebook.com

11. Where Did Facebook Come From, About Social Media, last modified June 22, 2009. http://personalweb.about.com/od/makefriendsonfacebook/a/whatisfacebook_5.htm

12. How Twitter was Born, 140 Characters, last modified 2012. http://www.140characters.com

CHAPTER 3

Julie Hirauk– "Babies and Boomers"

1. Does Google have a social media site?

2. Instigram is primarily used for sharing photos?

   True or False

3. What is Pintrest?

Ever since the Internet was invented, some kind of social media site has existed. In the beginning, it might just have consisted of exchanging e-mails with people at your work, now social media sites are endless, the most popular ones, Facebook and Twitter. There are also some other popular sites out there that people love being on. Along with these sites there are some new ones being invented, or old sites just starting to get noticed. No one really knows what the next big web site will be because it depends on what people are ready for if people will like it. Every year, sites fail because Internet users do not like the site or maybe the site is just not popular enought. Here are some web sites that are either just starting out or are just now becoming popular.

myYearbook

An old site that was somewhat popular when it first came out, but as time goes on more and more people are starting to join and are making it more popular, one site like this is myYearbook. In 2005, two high school students that decided to make their own yearbook because they did not like their high school yearbook so they founded myYearbook. They wanted it to be more than just a virtual yearbook, so the site allows its users create a profile and connect with other members. In some ways, myYearbook is similar to Facebook and Myspace, but there are also some differences.

Starting out on myYearbook is similar to starting out on Facebook because the user first has to build their own profile. This process starts with having a valid e-mail address and then the user will have to fill in their name, location, gender, and birthday. The user will also have to verify that he/she is an actual human being. Once all of the information is in the computer, a person can upload a picture of themselves so others can see who they are. With the upload of the photo the basic profile will be complete. After building a profile, the user can start searching for friends by using his/her own e-mail address book. A person can change his/her statuses, similar to Facebook and Twitter, but he/she can also create playlists, add video, television shows, and post blog entries to his/her profile. In addition to these features, there are games, quizzes, applications, and messages.

One way that myYearbook differs from Facebook and through its Lunch Money program. A user can earn Lunch Money by doing just about anything. The user starts earning Lunch Money by just creating an account, and continues to earn money by just logging onto the site, convincing others to join, finishing certain tasks, and winning battles. With the currency that a user collects, he/she can buy other members photos, donate the money to different causes, or can buy virtual presents for other members. MyYearbook also does something different from most sites, which is that members can battle each other with their photos. To do so people select a picture they have and put it up against someone else's and the myYearbook community will vote to see who has the better picture.

Google+

There are many companies and web site designers out there that are trying to out due other social media sites. For example to try and beat out Facebook, Google decided to make a new Social Media Site called Google+, an extension of Google itself. Google+ was first launched in June of 2011, but this was only to people who got an invitation. After this group the trial test was over and the site was open to anyone 18 or older in September of 2011. This social media site has many different features and can be confusing to use at first, but becomes easier with time.

These features include Stream, Sparks, Circles, Hangouts, Games and Photos. Stream is like your newsfeed on Facebook or Twitter. This feature just shows the user the activity of their friends. Sparks is a recommendation engine, which finds the user the most interesting news content related to the topic that they are searching. Just like on most other sites a Google+ user has friends, but on Google+ they have more control over what their friends can see and do on their profile. Within the friend list one can create different circles, and then choose who will be in those certain circles. Having this feature one can pick who gets to see certain information that the person might not want everyone else on their page to see. Hangouts are like Skype, but a person can do more in the Hangout setting then they can do on Skype. Hangouts let the user choose who will be able to join the video chat, either by individual or by circle. Once a certain person or group is chosen those people can join in whenever they are ready and up to ten people can video chat at once. These features give a person a different experience than they do on Facebook or Twitter.

To get started on Google+ a person must have a Gmail account. If someone has already created a Google profile, Google+ will recognize it and will just use all of that information, but if not the user will have to start with the basic information like your name and birthday. After these parts are filled out the user can put a brief description about yourself and choose a picture for your profile. Along with the normal information Google+ allows someone to add personal websites as well as Twitter and Facebook to the right of the page. A person can add an "Introduction," "Occupation," "Places Lived," "Relationship," "Nickname," and "Looking For." Google+ is like Facebook in many ways because it allows a person to put a lot of the similar information on their profile, but it also lets you put some different information on there too.

Pinterest

Most social media sites are about having a newsfeed and sharing your statuses with all your friends. Pinterest on the other hand is a little bit different. This social media site is all about pictures and pinning them onto different boards of you're choosing. When using Pinterest someone can browse others pins or boards and get ideas for different parts of their lives. One can either search everything or one can search by a certain categorie.

Getting started on Pinterest is also a little different because as of right now someone can only join by invite because it is a closed site. For this to happen one either needs to have Pinterest itself send them an invite, or get an invite from someone who is already a member of the Pinterest community. Then once the invite comes, one can get connected a couple different ways. A person can connect through their Facebook or Twitter accounts. Once signed in, one can change their username, biography, and profile picture if they so desire.

After all the basic information is settled a user will be able to start creating as many boards as they want and name them whatever their little heart desires. It is easy to look through the pins and find what one person likes and repin. A pin is just an image someone found on the Internet that they like and put it on Pinterest. Once someone sees a pin they like they can either like the pin, or they can repin it to one of their boards. With repining something a person adds that image to the board of their choice. By having these different boards a person can plan out different aspects of their life. For example if someone finds a certain food that they like, one can repin that to their board named food and then later they can go back to that pin and get the recipe from the web site. A person can also plan their wedding using Pinterest. A person can use Pinterest for a lot of different aspects in his/her life.

StumbleUpon

Another social unique social media site is StumbleUpon. This web site is similar to Pinterest in a way that a person can search for different information according to categories. Instead of looking through different pins, a person on StumbleUpon "stumbles" their interest. StumbleUpon helps you discover and share great web sites that a person would probably never find on their own.

For someone to get on StumbleUpon they have to sign up for a profile, but StumbleUpon is an open web site so anyone can join. Once the profile is set up a person can start picking different categories that they are interested in. After one's interest is picked they can begin to stumble, which simply means that different web sites that are within you interest will come up. Like Facebook there is a like button, but there is also a dislike button. With StumbleUpon a user is taken directly to web sites matching their personal interest and will not have to search through thousands of pointless sites. The nice part about StumbleUpon is that the different web sites come up with just a click of a button and the user does not have to do anything else.

Foursquare

Along with social media sites on the web there are also some that are mobile applications that have people going nuts. One of these applications is Foursquare. This site is a geographical location based social network, and incorporates gaming elements. This network allows a person to "check in" to certain locations. By checking in the user shares this information with his/her friends, but also with the Foursquare community. Checking in allows for a social map to be made that shows where certain people are and where they have been.

For a user to "check in" somewhere they need to use a mobile web site, text message, or the Foursquare application on their Smartphone. By checking into places the user is awarded points and sometimes badges. A user can start earning points by checking into a new site or a site that they have already been to. Someone can earn badges by checking into various venues, or in certain cities, it just depends on what and where the badge is. Also checking into a certain place so many times allows that person to become the "mayor" of that place. The only way this will occur is by checking into that one place more than anyone else. These are some of the features that makes Foursquare different from the big social media sites like Facebook and Twitter.

Flickr

There are a lot of social media sites on the web that are about finding out what people are doing or how they are feeling. Another way to find out what someone has been up to is by looking at their pictures. Some have even found pictures to be the easy way to "creep" on certain people. One web site that is just devoted to photos and videos is Flickr. Flickr is an image hosting and video hosting web site. With Flickr someone does not need an account to view others photographs, but an account is needed if someone would want to upload something to the web site. Having an account will allow one to have their own personal profile with the video and pictures that they have taken.

Just like any other social media site Flickr has some different features to make it its own. The first thing a new user will notice is that there is a Free version and there is a Pro version. With the Free one a user has a limited amount of space to put their photo up in a month, but the Pro version has an unlimited amount of space.

To make communication easier with other members that have the same interest, one can create a group. With the group the creator can manage what goes on within said group. Flickr also lets the person that uploaded pictures or video tag them. This feature can help some know where the photograph was taken or what the subject matter is. With using Flickr people can "creep" on just other people's photos and not have to deal with statuses.

Instagram

People do not have to have the big and fancy camera to post their pictures to different social media sites. There is an application (app) for iPhones, iPads, and iPod Touches that allows someone to post their pictures from these devices. The application is called Instagram. This is a free app that allows people to take a photo, apply a digital filter, and then share it on their choice of social media sites. There is also an application coming for Andriod sometime soon.

The social media sites that were mentioned in this chapter are just some of the new and upcoming sites or sites that are just now becoming popular. For most of the web sites someone has to have a profile and need some basic information from the user to get started. Some of the sites have to deal with having newsfeeds and changing one's status. Then there are others that one can see what someone is up to with viewing the pictures that they have put on their profile. Also one can search different sites by just what they like and do not have to worry about looking through nonsense. In today's constantly changing world no one can really predict what the next best social media site is going to be. One can only try and keep up with the Internet and what other people think is cool and interesting.

REFERENCES

Fitchard, Kevin. Foursquare seems silly, but it could be the future of information. N.p., 12 Nov. 2010 Accessed Feb. 20, 2012. <http://connectedplanetonline.com/mobileapps/news/Foursquare seems-silly-but-it-could-be-the-future-of-information-1112/>.

Parr, Ben. Google+: The Complete Guide. N.p., 16 July 2011. Accessed Feb. 20, 2012. <http://mashable.com/2011/07/16/google-plus-guide/>.

Pinterest. Pinterest Getting Started. N.p., 16 Sept. 2011. Accessed Feb. 20, 2012 <http://pinterest.com/about/help/>

Strickland, Jonathan. How myYearbook Works. N.p., 2010. Accessed Feb. 20, 2012 <http://computer.howstuffworks.com/internet/social-networking/networks/myyearbook.htm.>

StumbleUpon.About StumbleUpon. N.p., 2011. Accessed Feb. 20, 2012. <http://www.stumbleupon.com/aboutus/>

Wikipedia.Flickr. N.p., 27 Feb. 2012. Web. 28 Feb. 2012. <http://en.wikipedia.org/wiki/Flickr>.

Wikipedia. Foursquare (website). N.p., 26 Feb. 2012. Accessed Feb. 20, 2012. <http://en.wikipedia.org/wiki/Foursquare_(website)>

Wikipedia. Instagram. N.p., 27 Feb. 2012. Accessed Feb. 20, 2012. <http://en.wikipedia.org/wiki/Instagram>.

CHAPTER 4

Caroline Ghosn– "You Type a Big Game"

1. What can the lack of face to face contact lead to?

2. Social networking entices people to?

3. What are the benefits of social media?

Caroline Ghosn

You Type a Big Game

Introduction

Social media has significantly changed the way that people communicate with one another. Not too long ago, we communicated through the mail, on a land-line telephone, and in person. Now, with the evolution of technology and constant advancements these traditional forms of communication seem ancient to us. Although the popularity of a specific website may fade, online social networking is not just a trend. Rather, it is a new way of life that future generations, even generation Y, are becoming dependent on. My iPhone has been glorified fifth ligament for the past few years, allowing me to contact virtually anyone, anywhere, at any time via Facebook and Twitter apps. With social media here to stay people need to be aware of the positive and negative effects that it has on communication. Conflicting theories and research on the effects of media have sparked debates throughout the world about media as a growing social problem. A general assumption is that communication technologies help to increase and strengthen social ties. Some psychologists have argued that social media has both risks and benefits to children. Psychologists that study the effects of social media on children go as far as to say it can lead to the development of personality and social disorders. This chapter will be focusing on what I have found as the pros and cons of communication through the use of social media.

Emotional Ties

People tend to act a lot bolder and braver behind a computer screen, thus leading to exaggerated emotions. You can pretend to be whoever you want to be, in turn forming bonds with unsuspecting people. Many things said on social media sites, either good or bad, are never said in person because there is a computer screen to hide behind. The lack of face to face contact makes the communication between others indirect hence the outcome seems harder to associate to the actions. Not only do people's emotions become exaggerated, but their words become misinterpreted. A simple winky face or something written in all caps posted online can mean something different depending on who's reading it.

Anger: You find out that your ex is dating your friend through another friend. Without knowing the whole story you see something posted and automatically jump to conclusions. The most common reactions to something like this is going on Twitter or Facebook and retaliate in some way. Usually by posting a tweet like "She/he is a home wrecker, hope you like my leftovers." This scenario results in you taking your anger out on your friend without needing the confidence to say it in person. The outcome of tweets and posts like this tend to hurt people and can lead to cyber bullying. On the opposite end of the spectrum, you may see the post, get really angry and close your accounts. This leads you to withdraw from most of your other friends since these social media sites keep many people in constant touch.

Relationships: Boy meets girl. Girl does not get number but thinks boy is cute. For many, the next step is to monitor their every move and dig up their history. In reality, that is what many do through the use of Facebook and Twitter. Not only is it like they are stalking them slowly in their car but they also are time traveling back in time to monitor their activities from the past years. With the expansion of social media in this decade there is little information that is left private. All sorts of pictures get put up of places you have been and people you have been with including current and past boy/girlfriends. Relationships have suffered and ended because of the easy access to form emotional bonds with others. What may start as innocent chatting online is leading some people to start having deeper feelings and eventually acting on them. Nowadays when you meet someone you don't think twice about looking them up on social sites. Two people meet, are interested in one another, and begin dating. Since they have looked the other up, they already in a sense judged the other person. They saw and read things and interpreted them the way they wanted to, which may not be the truth. This is done by going through photo albums, posts, and statuses on Facebook which may seem like just ordinary actions but are creepy in a nonsocial media context.

Sadness: Tweet: I did not get that job I wanted #cryingmyeyesout

Facebook status: Boyfriend broke up with me, cannot eat or sleep hmu

Most people immediately post dramatic tweets that usually do not reflect their actions. They allow social media to exaggerate their emotions by posting it online and making the situation seem much worse than it actually is. In turn their posts and statuses provide them with a sympathetic and understanding audience. This allows them to receive a lot of attention since people become concerned in their business.

Hyper sexuality: There is no way to know if the information disclosed is accurate or truthful descriptions that is used when creating usernames on social media sites. As you click on Chatroulette, you meet people from all over the world or they can even happen to be your neighbors. The site allows you to video chat with randomly selected persons and if you do not wish to chat with them you can hit next and move on to another. But as you swap between people not only are you anonymous but so are the people on the opposite side of the screen. Some of these people could be strangers posing nude or doing sexual gestures on the screen. As crazy as this seems, it has tended to be the majority of the different people I have seen and none of the times has it been something I wanted to see. In general, I do not think many people go on Chatroulette to see that and are in for a surprise if they did not expect it. Many of the strangers that are showing their genitals would not be doing this if it was not for the screen between them and the receiver. The only connection is millions of proxy walls and other than that they are not linked to you. They would probably not be open to the idea of walking around in the mall and pulling their pants down at the sight of another person. In fact they would probably be arrested and committed to a psychiatric ward under suspicion of mania.

Connecting for Miles

Costly calling cards are products of the past. You no longer need to go through hassles to reach a country miles and miles away. It is as easy as logging onto Facebook, Twitter, or MySpace and sending a message that takes less than minutes. Social media sites allow you to stay in touch with relatives or friends that may live far away. They allow you to be part of their lives through posts and tweets allow that constantly update you about their life.

Reaching masses

A simple question, advice on getting your high school crush, dealing with a health issue, changing jobs, finding a new place to live, buying a car are all issues that can be posted and answered on social networks. Social networking sites can help connect you with friends and experts who can assist in your decision making process. For some people they receive advice on major life issues that previous to social sites they would have only had one source of advice.

Creative Expression

Communication does not have to take the form of words. People can communicate with one another through art. People with common interests are brought together through social media sites with different groups open to anyone who wants to join. Facebook, MySpace, YouTube, and Twitter can be used as a medium for creative expression. They provide free blogging, photo storage, video uploads, albums, photo editing tools, etc. Sites offer exposure to amateur artists spreading their work around the world. While many amateurs are nervous are nervous about showing their work to others, social media can lower inhibitions to overcome social anxiety.

Lingo

Social media sites have created a new language that has entered the social world. Smh at all the hw I hav due 2mr, its not kewl. Rather than stating, shaking my head at all the homework I have due tomorrow, it is not cool. Chat slang is a lot shorter and can come in handy when a quick messaged is needed to be written. Now it is not just prevalent on social media sites but also in the academic environment. Kids are using it to take notes in class or are quick to abbreviate words in papers. Grammar rules and writing skills are quickly being thrown out by the new generation and being replaced by Internet lingo.

Interaction

Social networking sites entice people to spend more time online and less time interacting face-to-face. The sites offer many time consuming activities that supplant more productive activities. The hours per day of face-to-face socializing have declined as the use of social media has increased. People who use these sites frequently are prone to social isolation. Parents spend less time with their children and couples spend less time together even when they live in the same house because they are using the Internet instead of interacting with each other. Perhaps it can also be argued that social media can actually increase a person's communication skills. There are people who have a hard time with direct contact and isolate themselves from human interaction. For some it might be that they are shy, others it might be that it is embarrassing and stressful to have direct communication with others. Social media provides a portal for these individuals to interact with others in an atmosphere that is a more comfortable.

Overview

The increasing dominance of social media on this world is too great to ignore. It is influencing every aspect of our lives especially the way we communicate. Like anything else these influences are both good and bad and we have to be aware of both. The screen of a computer separating individuals can lead to exaggerated emotions and misinterpreted messages. This is only in some cases that people use social media as a battle field. People can benefit from social sites by being able to connect to people that live far away. Although they are distant they are able to form a close connection through the use of social sites by seeing constant updates on what they have been doing. It is virtually an enhancing toolset we can use to communicate on a more global level. The intimate connection that takes place when people speak to one another in person is disappearing. It is being replaced with an in direct form of communication. Disappearing along with it is, spending quality family time, doing hands on activities with friends and face to face conversations. On the other hand, people who have difficulty communicating in person are more comfortable interacting through social media sites. As discussed throughout this chapter social media has caused the way we communicate to evolve in ways that are beneficial but also has a downside. The spread of social media will only increase with time hence we must embrace but with caution.

CHAPTER 5

Rebecca Olsavsky– "For Fans Only"

1. What 3 things are keys to successful information flow between businesses and fans?

2. How do businesses use social media to boost their credibility?

3. What are some of the rewards businesses offer to their social media fans and followers?

For Fans Only!: Social Media Marketing

C*lick*. Logging into my Facebook account, I quickly scroll down my newsfeed to check for any new pictures or interesting status updates posted by friends, then I get down to business. *Look, TLC posted a preview for tonight's episodes. And Target is offering a discount on DVDs.* Scrolling down a little further, I notice that Blush Makeup Artistry posted a link to OPI's latest nail polish collection, inspired by the NYC Ballet.[1] *Click.* A new window opens, and immediately I'm taken to the OPI web site, all thanks to Blush.

Local business owner Angela Taylor may have a small business in Blush, but the Wheeling Jesuit Business major takes her brand to a new level on Facebook and Twitter by using her pages as platforms for other brands in the same industry as her own. Basically, Taylor uses social media to connect her business to larger trends in the beauty industry. She still knows how to promote her own page, though. I fairly frequently get "Blush Makeup Artistry Open House" event invites containing special makeup deals for those who attend.

Social Media Marketing- What is it and why does it exist?:

Although Blush Makeup Artistry is an example of a local, small-scale business utilizing features of social media, beauty brands on a national scale realize the potential of social media marketing, using social media sites as platforms for promoting a brand, as well. For instance, Birchbox, a monthly subscription service offering beauty product samples, relies heavily on a variety of social media sites as a means of garnering both credibility and an expanding audience. Beyond the beauty world, industries of all kinds manage their social media marketing to constantly develop the information flow between brand and fan. Case in point: magazines like *TIME*, home shopping networks like QVC, and even discount retailers like Target work daily to perfect their management of Facebook, Twitter, and YouTube.

Today, virtually any local business, company, or big-name brand can be followed online by social media users. Why has this become standard? The reason is both complicated and simple. Social media's simple because it provides centralized channels for information flow. On the flip side, it's complicated because those centralized channels allow unlimited amounts of information to flow. For businesses, the key to successful information flow through social media involves focusing on three things that benefit both businesses and fans: sharing business updates, offering rewards, and promoting interaction with loyal customers. Let's look at those benefits up close.

Business Updates:

The first and foremost obvious reason businesses use social media is for updating fans. Sites like Facebook and Twitter equal instant connection to the public, so of course businesses and brands use social media to reveal "breaking news" about things like special events and upcoming products. Plus, businesses showcase their credibility as brands through social media by posting links to news in which they are referenced or rated.

Now, the whole brand-event combo is a smart move by businesses. Why? Whether it's a Facebook party or Twitter chat, event invitations from businesses via Facebook invite or tweet suggest an initiative on the part of the brand to personally connect to fans, reminding fans to check out their page. True, personal open house invites from small business Blush Makeup Artistry are personal, but big businesses can be personal, too. Organize.com, an online company selling home organization tools ranging from tool racks to coupon organizers, devotes its Facebook page to acting as a sort of forum or chat room where fans who are particularly chatty in interacting with other fans are rewarded with products from the brand's site. Last year, when Organize.com invited its now almost 20,000 fans to its "LIVE from the National Hardware Show Facebook Party!," over 250 fans agreed to log in to their accounts on May 11 and participate in a conversation on the brand's page from 3:00-5:00 p.m.[2] Having accepted the invite, I thought it was a really unique event because live online conversation was matched with a live physical event at the National Hardware Show. Even though the online event appeared to be about the fans, it really was a way for Organize.com to share its presence at the National Hardware Show with an attentive online audience waiting for rewards. I didn't win any prizes during the online event, but it was obvious that the Organize.com team running the Facebook party actually read through all of the comments to find the most interactive fans worthy of winning products.

Speaking of products, I come to my second point about updates. Another way businesses use social media is to promote upcoming products that have yet to hit the market. As the people following a brand's page are the ones most likely to care about its newest products because they likely are loyal fans, product updates via social media are an important tool for businesses to employ. Bath & Body Works, a self-described body care and home fragrance store, introduces new fragrances with every season; that means lots of social media updating. Take Twitter, for example. With almost 32,000 Twitter followers, Bath & Body Works can tweet, "Spotted! NEW Mango Cilantro Candles [*link to photo here*]. What's your favorite Spring/Summer fragrance?," and 32,000 newsfeeds will fill with the brand's update.[3] By adding a question to the product update, the business can to a certain extent monitor how many followers read the tweet by checking for @replies. The more @replies, the more the message spreads throughout other newsfeeds. So, followers of Bath & Body Works followers indirectly receive an update. It's all about connectivity.

Connectivity is definitely a major aspect of social media marketing, but so is credibility. That brings me to my third and final point for updates: businesses use social media to showcase their credibility as brands through displaying links to articles or news updates in which the business is referenced. This is especially important for businesses in service and education industries because, for these industries, the quality of people providing the service or education matters. Locally, Wheeling Jesuit knows the significance of posting links to outside news sources that positively promote the university. A major link for the university to post on its Twitter page included an article titled "Promoting Contemporary Jesuit Education Locally, Internationally and Globally," which was written by the president of the Association of Jesuit Colleges and Universities and discussed the value of a Jesuit education focused on service to others, no matter their location.[4] The link's source web site? Whitehouse. gov. With Wheeling Jesuit students making service trips to places like El Salvador, the article fit perfectly with the university's brand. Plus, because the White House has such a reputable, distinguished site, the fact that the university can make a connection to such a credible source is powerful.

Here's a review. Businesses and brands offer updates for three main reasons. First, they update fans, often while interacting with them, regarding special events. Second, they post updates to preview new products to loyal fans. Finally, they post links to outside sources that boost their credibility. With that, let's move on to rewards.

Rewards:

So far, I've mainly mentioned benefits from the perspective of the business. Shifting focus to the fans, it's obvious that social media marketing couldn't sustain itself without loyal fans liking, following, and subscribing to Facebook, Twitter, and YouTube pages. But, besides updates, what are the reasons fans keep up-to-date with a business online? There must be some kind of reward.

One of the most common rewards I've seen offered by a variety of businesses and brands includes things like special offers, discounts, and promotional, or "promo," codes.[5] By following businesses, fans can receive exclusive deals that people who don't keep up with social media may not be aware of or receive. For example, Posh Pouches, a small online business selling environmentally friendly reusable snack bags, sometimes offers an additional free snack bag with a purchase of $25 or more.[6] The catch is that you have to be a Facebook fan to get the deal. Here's another interesting use of special offers. CouponCabin, a site that already provides readers with discount-saving deals, bumps costs even more by providing Facebook fans with extra-exclusive promo codes that they can plug in to their checkout while ordering from online stores.[7] Loyalty is rewarded.

Saving money is always a great deal, but when brands offer big sweepstakes, giveaways, or contests for their followers, fans feel extra special. Usually, businesses conducting sweepstakes and contests ensure that the winner's prize is more of an experience relating to the brand than simply a lifetime product supply.[8] Because the idea of an experience prize, like a makeover or trip, lets the fan envision himself/herself as a winner, the whole concept seems more focused on the consumer than a self-promoting move by a business. By holding a Facebook sweepstakes entitled "MyLowe's Home Makeover," the home improvement store Lowe's offers fans a makeover experience in which Lowe's products will definitely be used, yet the tools aren't the ultimate end of the prize.[9] In the same type of move but through a different social media site, Cabela's, the outfitter for recreational activities like hunting, fishing, and camping, tweeted followers, asking, "Are you the @Cabela's Ultimate Outdoor Team?"[10] Below the question appeared a link to the contest's homepage and informational YouTube video. The prize, matching the brand's adventurous spirit, included a trip to New Zealand for two.

I'd have to agree that the sweepstakes' prizes are pretty special, but there's also something validating about simply being recognized by a favorite brand. Businesses and brands must know this, because some reward fans who actively contribute to their social media page by featuring them. Features can be anything from being awarded "fan of the week" or being published in the comments section of a magazine. The Facebook page for Fox's musical comedy, Glee, contains a tab for fans to submit their name and comment to become the "GLEEk of the Week." GLEEks' names and Facebook or Twitter photos are shown on screen at the end of every Glee episode.[11] For *Better Homes and Gardens* magazine, the traditional letters to the editor have been combined with fans' Facebook posts.[12] Posting a "letter to the editor" is much faster than writing a letter or an email to the magazine. Plus, the magazine most likely receives a broader demographic response by including social media. More comments mean it's more special to be featured, as well.

Remember, businesses still need a purpose in offering all of these rewards. When loyal fans advertise the brand by word of mouth (or word of "mouse," as it's now known in the age of social media), and when businesses "Like" each other's pages in a way of co-marketing with one another, brands benefit from free advertising through the work of people outside the business. As I mentioned earlier, connectivity is important for social media marketing. When fans feel like they're getting something from following a brand online, they're likely to increasingly interact with that brand's social media page, which leads to a greater online presence for the brand.

Interaction:

So far, the common thread running through everything I've mentioned is interaction. For businesses to successfully update and reward fans, fans need to be willing to offer their time in return through entering contests and commenting on news. The interactive nature of social media marketing ultimately benefits both parties because, with more interaction, both groups can have a better understanding of the other beyond face value.

Let's face it; when customers think of businesses, they think of entities, not people. For businesses, using social media can humanize a brand by adding a "face to the name" when that business devotes a team of social media experts to manage the brand's online interaction with fans.

Fans love when a brand's social media team tweets them back or replies to their comments. Plus, by interacting with fans through replying to comments, a business can discover details about its target market on an individual basis. The interaction initiative can shift back over to fans when they control how they are perceived as a target market by participating in polls. For example, notebook brand Five Star® asks fans in their target market, including a younger generation attending school, interesting poll questions like "Which of these Grammy nominees for the Record of the Year do you rock out to on your way to school?"[13] Those fans who interact by answering the polls will reap the reward of having advertising, products, or services by the brand be better tailored to their interests and style.

Besides interacting with a brand's social media team, fans of the brand connect with other fans and develop an online community. Within that online community, fans can use a brand's social media page as a way to give feedback to both the business and other fans of the brand. Basically, Facebook and Twitter are customer service and reviews in one. The customer service type of interaction also tests the business' willingness to address problems with its products.[14] Coffee company Starbucks isn't afraid to own up to any issues. On its Twitter page alone, the brand answers numerous tweets of complaint about service, but it does so in such a friendly and helpful way that it benefits them more than harms.[15]

Another thing that the online community enjoys discussing is common interests. As fans and brand share interest in an industry dependent on what the brand sells, it's common for businesses to use social media to discuss industry trends through providing links to current news relating to the business' industry. Birchbox, a beauty product sample subscription service, is always posting, tweeting, and offering "how-to" video links to the latest beauty industry trends.[16]

Interaction, whether focused on the big industry picture or the smallest product detail, is what keeps social media marketing a success. The layers of interaction allow businesses to learn about their target market and provide fans with the opportunity to voice their opinions. This back-and-forth interaction makes things easier for both groups.

Conclusion:

When consumers scrolling through their newsfeeds read a link to an article or promo code for a discount that a brand's posted, social media marketing seems easy. But as Angela Taylor of Blush Makeup Artistry knows, constant business planning and social media maintenance are vital for a brand to thrive in the online world. If done successfully, social media can be a brand's best friend. With benefits, including business updates, rewards, and interaction, for both brands and fans, it's not surprising that there are so many businesses utilizing the limitless tools of social media.

REFERENCES

1. Blush Makeup Artistry. Facebook. Accessed February 15, 2012. https://www.facebook.com/organizecom#!/blushmakeupartistryco.

2. Organize.com. Facebook. Accessed February 15, 2012. https://www.facebook.com/organizecom.

3. Bath & Body Works. Twitter. Accessed February 15, 2012. http://twitter.com/#!/LUVBBW.

4. Wheeling Jesuit. Twitter. Accessed February 15, 2012. http://twitter.com/#!/WheelingJesuit.

5. "Deal with It! Discounts Drive Brand Love on Social Media." The Nielson Company. Last modified November 3, 2011. *http://blog.nielsen.com/nielsenwire/global/deal-with-it-discounts-drive-brand-love-on-social-media./*

6. Posh Pouches. Facebook. Accessed February 15, 2012. https://www.facebook.com/pages/Fans-of-Posh-Pouches/.

7. CouponCabin. Facebook. Accessed February 15, 2012. https://www.facebook.com/CouponCabin.

8. Arnold, John. "How to Create a Social Media Sweepstakes or Contest." Entrepreneur Media, Inc. Last modified December 1, 2010. *http://www.entrepreneur.com/article/217659.*

9. Lowe's Home Improvement. Facebook. Accessed February 15, 2012. https://www.facebook.com/lowes.

10. Cabela's. Twitter. Accessed February 15, 2012. http://twitter.com/#!/Cabelas.

11. Glee. Facebook. Accessed February 15, 2012. https://www.facebook.com/#!/Glee.

12. *Better Homes and Gardens.* Facebook. Accessed February 15, 2012. https://www.facebook.com/#!/mybhg.

13. Five Star®. Facebook. Accessed February 15, 2012. https://www.facebook.com/#!/
FiveStar.

14. Falls, Jason, and Erik Deckers. "How to Use Social Media for Research and
Development." Entrepeneur Media, Inc. Last modified December 7, 2011. *http://www.entrepreneur.
com/article/220812*.

15. Starbucks Coffee. Twitter. Accessed February 15, 2012. http://twitter.com/#!/
StarBucks.

16. Birchbox. Birchbox. Accessed February 15, 2012. http://birchbox.com.

CHAPTER 6

Whitney Young– "Fear the Cookie Monsters"

1. How do companies advertise directly to me?

2. What is the easiest way to determine if something is a scam?

3. How many people per year fall victim to scams?

Fear the Cookie Monster

How do you contact people? Get the news? Find entertainment? There's one undoubtable answer in today's world, the Internet. People use the Internet for hours throughout the day, sending e-mails, playing games, using social networks, etc. Do you ever stop to think about some of the components that make the web so entertaining, annoying, or even dangerous? Read along to learn how businesses have come to use the Internet to their advantage, such as targeted advertisements. Targeted advertising is a type of advertising in which companies attempt to reach their consumers based on different qualities like observed behavior, demographics, and purchase history. This technology has opened a gateway for companies to reach consumers and potential customers in a quick and effective manner. This chapter will also answer some questions, including "How does my computer know I shop at that store?" "Is it solely based from information a person types into his or her computer? And most importantly this chapter covers the dangers of surfing the web and opening mysterious links.

Targeted adverting has allowed companies to receive feedback from consumers at such a rapid pace that it has phased out the use of surveys. Surveys were considered to be the most effective way of discovering statistics, opinions, and gaining feedback. They were also thought to be the quickest way to help a company locate their strengths and weakness. Although surveys are still widely used by companies, the new technology of targeted adverting has proved more successful. Surveys seemed to lack in many areas that targeted advertisements proved more helpful. When surveys were administered, consumers did not answer correctly or with much information. Companies could not get a precise statistic or gain much knowledge from the survey. Surveys that were mailed to the consumers seemed to have multiple problems, such as low response rates. The response rate includes the number of people who answered the survey divided by the number of people in the sample. This posed a problem for companies because a low response rate meant their consumers were not answering or giving feedback. Also, a low response rate can contribute to sample bias. Sample bias is when a survey is collected and all members of the intended population are less likely to be included. This becomes a problem because all of the survey responses are not equally included or accounted for and the results are jeopardized. Another problem was how time consuming it could be to take a survey. Many times, consumers either avoid or do not take because they do not have the incentive to do so. Therefore, in order to keep the consumer's attention, the surveys were shortened, which made it harder to gain enough information. This meant there had to be another solution in receiving a quick and easy response from consumers, which would prove to be targeted adverting.

Targeted adverting allows businesses to personally talk to consumers online. Now companies pay employees to sit by a computer and respond to consumers and potential customers. Especially with sites such as Facebook and Twitter, companies can now talk to potential clients and previous customers first-hand on the Internet. Twitter, companies have employees read every tweet related to their product and respond to the customers via the site. Jacob Totherow, a student from Wheeling Jesuit University, was nice enough to give his story about a personal experience with twitter. Totherow is a frequent buyer of the Nike store. He bought a pair of running shoes expecting to be satisfied just like every other time with the product, however this time was different. The material of the shoe did not seem to last or hold up as well after wearing them only a couple times like the shoes he had previously bought from Nike. Totherow, upset about the purchase, tweeted to the Nike twitter page. He sent in a picture of the shoes and told them he was not satisfied with the quality of his purchase. The Nike store tweeted him fairly quickly and apologized for the inconvenience and poor quality of the shoes. A week or two later, Totherow received new shoes from the Nike store. The technique of targeted adverting proved to be helpful and quick. Not only are companies using targeted advertisements to their advantage but the consumers are finding it helpful and effective as well.

Do you ever wonder how companies personally target you? Based on keywords, sites visited, or information typed into the computer, you create a digital footprint. A digital footprint is a traceable path a person leaves behind online. This is the digital information transmitted online due to videos and pictures uploaded, e-mails, registration, usage of TV, and mobile phones. A person's digital footprint can be tracked or traced by anyone online. Based on what a person types into his or her search bar leaves a digital trail that can be traced by companies. Companies, support groups, or even schools can trace these paths to target a consumer. The reason companies are able to trace a person's path is because of cookies. A cookie is also known as a web cookie or browser cookie; it is used as a source website to send information to the owners computer browser and for the browser to be able to retune the information back to the source site. An Internet browser eats up hundreds of these cookie-tracking devices each time a site is visited. These cookies can be stored on a computer for up to a year which allows companies to monitor and track information.

A local student from Wheeling Jesuit University named Erin Metzger has often wondered how her computer targets her so well. When she logs on to Facebook, she sees ads for stores from her hometown in Canton, Ohio. "It's almost like my computer knows where I'm from," says Metzger. Although cookies are helpful when visiting sites, they mostly keep track of what a person does online. Since cookies trace a person's every move online, the Internet allows ad firms to follow whenever he or she moves from site to site. Over a period of time, the sites that have been visited allow companies to build a demographic profile based on activities, schools, place of residence, and income levels. Once the company has assembled a satisfactory profile on a person, it can target them directly. For example, if a person has visited a specific site multiple times, such as a university, cookies allow ad firms to see and track the moves made on the site. Possibly in the next few years when a person gets on the web the advertisements may show items that can be purchased from that university. This is one of the ways companies are able to trace and target a particular person. It allows companies to build a personal resume of someone without his or her knowledge. It is one of the best ways for companies to find their consumers.

Although cookies are not harmful to the computer, they do open a person's computer up for the world to track; so it is important to watch what sites are being visited. Also it is good to occasionally go to one's settings and clean the browser and get rid of some cookies. Based on the sites visited, a person's computer can be at high risk for scams and other harmful viruses to the computer. A scam is a scheme or a fraud. Scams are normally appealing or alluring ideas to get people to give money or to meet someone in person. Scams are one of the most important things to recognize. They can be very harmful to a computer and potentially cause it to crash. Not only is it harmful to a computer but it is also very dangerous for a person. Falling into scams can cause viruses, the loss of money, or in extreme cases, death. Scams are something to be very cautious about when surfing the web, from children's and adult sites. They can come in all sorts of forms, including messages, links, and pop-ups. They can pop-up as e-mails, a link on Facebook or Twitter, or a real person from another computer. It is important to be familiar with all types of scams and learn to avoid opening them.

First it is important to learn how to recognize a scam, here are the top five types of scams:

- Phishing Scams are e-mails. These are the scams that show up in your inbox once a person has opened his or her e-mail account. These types of messages normally have some type of financial connection to them. They usually have something to do with banking, which tells a person that something has gone wrong in his or her account and a change needs to be done quickly. This type of scam is used to get a person to give bank account information.

- Nigerian scams, are another type of e-mail. These messages state that the sender is very rich needs help trying to move money out of the country. In return, he or she will pay the person a large sum of money. This also is a scam to get bank account information.

- Holiday greeting cards are types of messages sent on a special holiday claiming they're from "a friend" with a cute message and song playing attached to them. Once you've clicked on the link to open the message, the computer directs you to another site or asks to install a video plug-in to view. Be careful for this type of scam because it is used to install a type of virus to damage the computer.

- Auction fraud is normally on bidding sites. A person bids and wins on an item but once the money is received, the merchandise is never sent. This is the second most reported fraud and it is very hard to distinguish it as a scam. The most important thing a person can do to avoid this type of scam is to read references and talk to previous winners from the person auctioning off item.

- Identity Thief Protection is a type of scam in which the scam artist pretend to be a company protecting people from identity thief. They make the customers believe they are working with a company in effort to get customers to give out bank account numbers, names, phone numbers, and family members. To stay protected, you must never give too much personal information out over the phone. Make sure a company has reliable sources, and always meet in person when something concerns banking information.

- You've Won A Prize, is a type of scam that can be online or over the phone. When online, it's best to ignore and not open the link. When a potential scam artist calls, never give out information over the phone, iinstead ask for a report sent to your home. Even then, it's important to check to make sure it's from a legitimate company.

Some of these scams can even be found on seemingly friendly sites like Facebook and Twitter. Most of the scams are claimed to be sent from "a friend" wanting a person to look at a video or open some type of link. If things seem strange or "too good to be true" online then they're probably not worth the trouble. The best ways to stay safe from scams are to ignore any potential messages or links that do not look normal.

There are countless numbers of scams out there. Most of them seem to focus on getting money. However, that does not include all types. There are many types of scams that try to convince someone to meet in person. Also, there are types of frauds that offer to sell things and meet up. These are the scams that especially need to be approached with caution. Many of these scams can lead to theft, sexual assault, or even death. Take the "Craiglist Killer" for example. Philip Markoff, also known as the "Craigslist Killer," was suspected of armed robbery and the murder of a woman. Markoff would look his victims up online and ask to meet with them privately and then rob them. These scam artists and potential killers are found on entrusted sites, which make it very difficult to tell if it is a scam. To avoid these types of risks, the best thing to do is meet in public places, during the day, and possibly with another person present.

Anyone can fall into scams at any point. That's why it is important to be well educated on what scams may look or sound like. Not everyone who falls into a scam is unaware of frauds. There are many things that contribute to a person falling into a scam, such as what's going on in a person's life at the time, if he or she is vulnerable, or sometimes someone can just be a little to greedy. For example, MSNBC TV anchor Contessa Brewer fell into a phishing scam and ended up giving away her social security number. She told reporters that she was in the process of moving and filling out dozens of forms. In the midst of all the chaos, she had a lapse of judgment and fell directly into a scam. No matter the person or the situation, everyone is at high risk. Typical victims include people who are lonely in hopes of doing something dramatic to improve their lives. Greedy people are typical victims due to the fact that they want to gain more and normally do not get a second opinion before making big decisions. The most common victim to scams includes old-aged adults. Most of the time, they do not recognize the scam itself since scams are changing at a rapid pace. It is important to always be aware of scams and not to think you will never fall victim.

When it comes to protecting one's self from scams and other viruses, it is important to keep a few things in mind. Recognize when something does not look normal. Do not open links just because "a friend" sends them. Do not open links from unheard of companies. When meeting someone, stay in public. It is also good to change your password from time to time. If pop-ups seem to come up more than try going to privacy settings on your computer and adjusting.

REFERENCES

1. Totherow, Jacob A. Interview by Whitney Young. Written. April 1, 2012.
2. Google. "My Digital Footprint." Accessed Feb. 25, 2012. http://blog.mydigitalfootprint.com/google-brain-are-we-losing-our-memory-to-the.
3. Metzger, Erin M. Interview by Whitney Young. Written. April 12, 2012.
4. Indiana University. "What Are Phishing Scams and How Can I Avoid Them?" Accessed Feb. 28, 2012. http://kb.iu.edu/data/arsf.html.
5. Bankrate. "15 Ways to Protect Yourself from Scams." Accessed Feb. 29, 2012. http://www.bankrate.com/brm/news/advice/20021025c.asp.

CHAPTER 7

Audra Macri– "Dress Your Page for Success"

1. How private should my pages are set to?

2. What are good social media practices in the offices?

3. Do companies really check Facebook before they hire?

As of January 2012 over eight percent of American Citizens are unemployed and currently seeking jobs. With the job market being more competitive than ever, potential employees must not only excel in the work place but also in their life outside of the office. In today's society it is almost impossible to live a "private" life. News travels like wildfire not only through talk but also through our social media profiles on Facebook, Twitter and even LinkedIn. By posting our life stories online we have given not only our friends access to our lives but the public in general whether we approve or not. However, this also sets us up for giving a bad impression of ourselves to the public which can also harm our professional life.

Potential employers use social media as a type of "free background check" to know what their possible employees do outside of the office. Many are finding it difficult to even get an interview due to the information that has been posted online about them, including Facebook statuses, pictures and Twitter posts. If someone is hired then the issue of using social media in the workplace becomes a bigger issue; when is it appropriate and when could you risk losing your job because of the time you spend on social media sites? We no longer live in a world where we have the luxury of keeping everything to ourselves; because of this, it is important to monitor our online footprint before, during and even after the job application process.

Believe it or not, the concept of social media affecting your professional life can happen to anyone. Today, it is very popular for potential employers to run a Google Search on your name before you are even called for an interview. Seventy-five percent of recruiters are required by their companies to do online research of candidates. Seventy percent of these same recruiters in the United States reported rejecting candidates because of information online (Preston). In 2006 a Louisiana State University student went to apply for a job, "During the interview, something he was not prepared for happened. The interviewer began asking specific questions about the content on his Facebook profile and the situation became very awkward and uncomfortable. The student had thought that only those he allowed to access his profile would be able to do so. The interviewer explained that as a state agency, recruiters accessed his Facebook account under the auspices of the Patriot Act" (Kennedy).

In a world where we have freedom of speech anything is fair game and unfortunately we must all be prepared to explain our actions. For example, one prospective employee was found using Craigslist to look for OxyContin. In another case a woman posing naked in photos she put up on an image-sharing site did not get the job offer she was seeking at a hospital. Other background reports have turned up examples of people making anti-Semitic comments and racist remarks (Preston). Unfortunately, our personal lives do tend to fall into our professional lives from time to time.

Many people see running a Google Search or hiring a company to run social media background checks as a breach of privacy, especially when the possible employee does not know a search will be conducted.

In February 2011 Microsoft performed a survey regarding how online reputations affect candidacy for employment and internships. The survey showed the following: Most recruiters and Human Resource professionals check online sources to research potential candidates. Seventy percent rejected candidates based on the information they found online, and eighty-five percent said that positive online reputation influenced their hiring decisions to some extent (Babbitt). One of the main reasons companies perform these searches is to protect not only themselves but also their organization by mitigating risks through due diligence and exercising a distinguished degree of care when it comes to job candidates and clients (Kennedy). Employers not only want to know that you are qualified to handle a job but that you also have the capability to not let your personal life effect the job you are hired to do.

Many people question why companies even take the time to search for someone online. Some see it as a breach of privacy, while others would prefer to be judged by their professional skills rather than their personal life. A recent article printed by The Wall Street Journal wrote about a company by the name of Union Square Ventures who had a job opening for an investment analyst. Instead of requesting for resumes or portfolios to be sent in, the venture-capital firm asked applicants to send links representing their "web presences" such as a Twitter account or a blog. Applicants also had to submit a short video demonstrating their interest in the position. Christina Cacioppo, an associate at Union Square Ventures, says "a resume doesn't provide much depth about a candidate… we are most interested in what people are like, what they are like to work with, and how they think."

John Fischer, the founder and owner of StickerGiant.com says a resume is not the best way to determine whether a potential employee will be a good social fit for the company (Silverman). Social media background checks have become so popular that there are even companies that can be hired out just for the very purpose of running social media background checks on potential employees. Social Intelligence is a year-old start-up company which scrapes the Internet for everything prospective employees may have said or done online in the past seven years (Preston). With the rise in online presence vs. professional skills, it is now more important than ever that we take into account what we put online and how it can affect other aspects of our life.

What we post on social media can not only affect our lives after college but also before and during our college careers. Most students today believe their Facebook account is personal property and they can say or do anything there without any consequences. Well, surprise! Believe it or not, there have already been several acts punishing students on college campuses and some even denying admission because of posts and pictures students have uploaded to the Internet. For example; one college applicant was denied admission in part because of his blog on LiveJournal. The Admission Dean said the student's blog, which was brought to his attention, included seemingly hostile comments about certain college officials. Swimmers at Louisiana State criticized coaches on Facebook and were kicked off the team. A high school freshman in Maryland was reportedly suspended because of online photos. Police busted an underage drinking party at George Washington University after they found invitations online (Verardi). In situations like these we think to ourselves, "How could someone be that stupid to even post that?" However, it is not a matter of personal rights or even freedom of speech. What needs to be considered before posting anything online is how a comment, picture or status will reflect not only on me personally but also on the organizations and businesses I am associated with.

While conducting research for this chapter, I came across many different pieces of advice on what to do in order to protect yourself from missing out on an employment opportunity due to social media. No one summed it up so perfectly, or as bluntly as an anonymous writer on a public forum, "Everything is public. Act as though it is going to be on the front page of the New York Times tomorrow." Any social media application you authorize is set to "Everyone" unless you specifically go to each application's privacy setting and change the settings. Any page that you "Become a Fan" of or group that you join on social networks is set to "Everyone" and may be displayed with your public profile page. The privacy settings for every comment you make to a fan or group page is controlled by the page or group, not by your personal privacy settings (Huffman).

Many job search engines offer several tips on how to make your social media profile ready for your job hunt. One of the best places to start is by "Googl-ing" your name to see what information is out there about you. You can then backtrack any questionable information you find and work to remove it from certain cites. Never post personal information such as your address, daily schedule, or phone number. Be sure to go into your privacy settings on all of your social media accounts so that strangers cannot look at your information, and be cautious about adding new friends who you do not personally know. Take down any questionable photos or exchanges between you and your friends. Give it the "Grandma Test." If you wouldn't want your grandmother to see it, then you don't want other adults to either. Remember, pictures and references of you on your friends' pages can be damaging too. You can ask them to remove this kind of information. Don't get a false sense of security on social media sites. It's easy for faculty, alumni and random people to get on and look at the information you have posted (Verardi).

After we have gone through the stressful task of applying for a job, interviewing and hopefully landing our dream job, we now have to consider how social media truly affects our day to day tasks at work. Let's face it, we have all been at work stuck in front of our computers, and the day seems like it is dragging on forever. We cannot help but "stumble" onto Facebook or Twitter and see what our friends are up to. Often I find myself searching for a YouTube video just to get some motivation back in me. But where does the line between being on social media just to take a quick break, and being on social media to the point where it affects our work performance begin and end.

The majority of us are familiar with the recent celebrity news about how Charlie Sheen was fired from his very popular television show due to the fact that he made public rants on social media outlets about his job and those he worked with. However, it is not just celebrities who get caught up in the dark side of social media; it can happen to anyone including students and employees in the Ohio Valley. Believe it or not one wrong post can send you on your way out of an institution. Even the amount of time you spend on social media during work hours is noted by employers and can result in negative consequences.

Employers will always be challenged by their employees with distractions from the outside world. Now that we live in a society where we can access any piece of social media or online information from the palm of our hands, it is even more difficult to regulate employees. First and foremost, employers should develop a social media policy. This policy should make clear to employees that it retains the right to monitor all use of its technology and any communications made or received on employer equipment ranging from office-based hardware to employer-provided cell phones. According to the decision of the National Labor Relations Board, employers have the ability to impose a complete ban on employee use of employer technology for personal or non-business communications (Lyncheski). Some companies have the option of even blocking certain social media websites if they believe it to be necessary. However, this solution does cost money and only applies to the computers used at the desk and not smart phones or other devices. The best thing an employer can do is set ground rules from the beginning on what they expect from their employees when it comes to social media. An employer should also work to set a good example and to quickly point out if there is a problem rather than letting it get out of control.

A safe place to start is to NOT become friends with your boss on Facebook or any other social media network. If you are going to take the time to post a status or tweet that bashes your job or your boss, more than likely they will see it and make note of it. In August 2009 a woman posted on her Facebook page - "OMG I HATE MY JOB!! My boss is a total pervvy (sic) w**ker, always making me do s**t stuff just to p**s me off!! W**ker!" The boss responded with a few comments of his own, ending with - "And lastly, you also seem to have forgotten that you have two weeks left on your six-month trial period. Don't bother coming in tomorrow. I'll pop your forms in the post and you can come in whenever you like to pick up any stuff you've left here. And yes, I'm serious." (Farrell).

A Cisco study revealed that more than twenty-five percent of employees admit to having changed the settings on their workplace computer to circumvent employer communication policies (Lyncheski). Many employers will not allow their employees to become friends with them through social media portals because of the ramifications of such acts as the one described above. Employers also feel that they must set an example by not constantly being on their social media profiles throughout the day. By doing this they have set guidelines without forcing employees to stick to them. It is also important for employees to do the same. Instead of hopping on Facebook every time you need a break, get away from your desk and walk around the building for a few minutes to clear your head, or grab a cup of coffee. By getting up and moving around you are not only reenergizing yourself, but you are also preventing yourself from falling into the black hole known as social media.

We live in a world where our personal and professional lives are intertwined. Employers take the time to run background searches for you online. Not only cleaning the skeletons out of your closet, but also making sure your personal life will not interfere with your professional career. Potential employers do not want to put their confidence in a loose cannon but rather make the hiring choice that will work out best of their company in the long run. Once you are hired, it is just as important to continue to keep your social media life clean and respectful. It is important to remember that your social media profile not only represents yourself but also the company you work for. Always keep in mind that information you post can be accessed as long as someone has enough determination and drive to get to it. The best advice I can give overall, "If you would not want your Mom or you Grandma to see it, you probably should not be posting it."

REFERENCES

1. Babbitt, Mark. "Is Your Online Reputation Affecting Your Career?." Classroom to Cubical. N.p., 11 Jan. 2011. Web. 12 Feb. 2012. <http://classroomtocubicle.com/finding-landing/internship/is-your-online-reputation-affecting-your-career/>.
2. Farrell, Rachel. "8 Ways to Get Fired Because of Social Media." Career Rookie. N.p., June 2010. Web. 4 Feb. 2012. <http://www.careerrookie.com/Article/CB-221-The-Real-World-8-Ways-to-Get-Fired-Because-of-Social-Media/>.
3. Huffman, Brenda K. "How Social Media Posts Can Affect Your Job Search." AXcessNews. N.p., 12 Feb. 2012. Web. 15 Feb. 2012. <http://axcessnews.com/index.php/articles/show/id/19850>.
4. Kennedy, Nicole, and Matt Macko. "Social Networking Privacy and Its Effects on Employment Opportunities." 9 Jan. (2011). Print.
5. Lyncheski, John E. "Social media in the workplace." Long Term Living Magazine Oct. 2010: 32-35. Web. 1 Mar. 2012. <http://search.ebscohost.com/login.aspx?direct=true&AuthType=ip&db=afh&AN=67443563&site=ehost-live>.
6. Preston, Jennifer. "Social Media History Becomes a New Job Hurdle." New York Times 20 July 2011. Web. 1 Mar. 2012. <http://www.nytimes.com/2011/07/21/technology/social-media-history-becomes-a-new-job-hurdle.html?_r=1&pagewanted=all>.

7. Silverman, Rachel E. "No More Resumes, Say Some Firms." The Wall Street Journal 24 Jan. 2012 [New York City] . Print.

8. Verardi, Nicole. "Social Networking and College Admission." National Association for College Admission Counseling. N.p., Apr. 2010. Web. 12 Feb. 2012. <http://www.nacacnet.org/PublicationsResources/steps/Articles/Pages/MySpace.aspx>.

CHAPTER 8

Brandi Richards– "Not So Picture Perfect"

1. If I report a picture can they see who reported it?

2. What Facebook application enables approval of tagged photos posted by a user's friend?

3. Aside from flagging the media, what else can one do to report inappropriate Twitter photos?

1.) Introduction

So, your current boyfriend just saw that photo of you and your ex-boyfriend at that party you lied about going to last month. Also, your boss just caught a glimpse of your all-too-obvious drunkenness at the local bar this past weekend on Facebook. Now you're single AND unemployed. Looks like you're batting 1000 this morning! Welcome to the world of incriminating photos, you newbie, where any photo with even the slightest hint of controversy posted on social media sites can and will be used against you in virtually every aspect of your life.

2.) What Does "Incriminating" Even Mean?

The technical definition of incriminating as defined by Dictionary. com is "to accuse of or present proof of a <u>crime</u> or fault."[1] Technical is not really what we are striving for here, though, so I will try my best to make my definition of incriminating as practical and relative to social media sites as possible. Incriminating, in my own sort of lamens terms, will now be defined as any photo on any social media site that holds the potential for the loss of a relationship, a job, a friendship, or really anything else that any ordinary person my give some value to.

While the aforementioned definition of incriminating is agreed upon by virtually everyone, I'm sure, what sort of photos could actually be considered incriminating is often disputed. For example, one person may see a photo of a woman wearing an under-21 band while seated atop a bar with a beer in each hand as totally permissible while another person might regard the very same photo as trashy. An absolute agreement on what kinds of photos are unmistakably incriminating will probably never be reached. However, it is safe to say that most people consider under-age drunken photos, age-appropriate yet unreasonably drunken photos, nude photos, and photos with exes while currently dating someone else as incriminating. I will shed some light on each of the previously mentioned examples of incriminating photos in the preceding paragraphs.

Underage Drunken Photos

Nothing says "incriminating" quite like a beer bottle in your hand and an under-21 band on your wrist. Make sure photos like these do not find their way to the various social media sites; the consequences are often pretty harsh for things that are illegal, like blowing up a building or stealing someone's car (not exactly the same, but close enough).

Age-Appropriate yet Unreasonably Drunken Photos

You probably won't end up behind bars if a picture like this makes its way to the internet. Plus, I doubt you would even lose a job or any sort of significant relationship. The worst that could happen is a little loss of dignity, but who needs or even knows what that is anyway?

Nude Photos

While the previous categories can be somewhat permissible in certain situations, I don't know of anyone who would classify a naked picture as anything but incriminating. Generally, people do not intend for nude photos to end up in realm of social media, yet cases of poor judgment and occasional intoxication often lead to them winding up there. Steer clear of posting fully or even partially nude pictures distastefully onto social media sites.

Photos with an Ex

Nothing says "I love you" quite like a picture of your current boyfriend or girlfriend with an arm slung around his or her past significant other. While there are generally no legal ramifications in these situations (granted the picture's inhabitants are fully clothed), the personal consequences can be just as bad. Seeing as these personal consequences can be extremely harsh, some people would probably choose doin' a little time in the slammer over listening to his or her partner complain about what he or she found of you on Facebook.

3.) "Don't tag me in that!"

Picture this: it's a Monday morning. You had a killer Saturday night at the local bar and may have gotten a little too carried away with your alcoholic intake, inclining you to partake in an overly embarrassing photo shoot with your best friend. Your friend, clearly experiencing a temporary lapse of judgment at the time, posted the photos on Facebook and Twitter and tagged you in all twenty of them. Now what? You have a few options, so don't freak out yet. Let me help you through this.

Approving and Removing Tags on Facebook

Some recent Facebook updates may save you from your current predicament. As is different from just a few years ago, there is now a setting on this social media monster that enables approval of a tagged photo before it automatically appears on user's page. However, the setting isn't automatic and must be turned on in a section of the site's privacy settings.

To access the profile review application, locate the drop-down "menu" tab in the top right corner of the page and find the "privacy settings" beneath it. From there, click "manage how tags work," "change settings," and turn the "profile (timeline) review" on. Profile review application on or not, photos tagged of you by non-Facebook friends require approval before their appearing your page.

For those of you without the profile review application turned on, photos tagged by friends are automatically added to your profile. A tag can certainly be removed from a photo. The "remove tag" action can be found under the symbol at the top right corner of the picture. Once a tag is removed from a particular photo, it will no longer appear on a user's profile. However, personally removing a tag has no effect on the photo's existence on the original poster's page or album.[2]

Marking your Media on Twitter

Twitter is not nearly as photo-driven as Facebook. In fact, I have had a Twitter account for nearly a year now and have uploaded one picture, and that was only to ensure that my followers would no longer see me as an egg. By the way, for clarity's sake, the "egg" I just mentioned represents the default photo that automatically appears on your personal Twitter page until you feel inclined to change it. Anyway, photos uploaded to Twitter are not able to be tagged as they are on Facebook. Twitter fanatics often mention a friend (or "follower") in the description of the photo instead.

Users of this social media site can take precautionary measures as a means of warning their followers of photos or videos they may post in the future. Confused? Well, let me clarify what I am referencing. If you plan to upload inappropriate types of media that are likely to offend your followers, see the "Settings" tab beneath the drop-down menu at the top right corner of the page. About halfway down the page will be a section called "Tweet media" that contains two options with checkboxes available. The second of the two checkboxes will read "Mark my media as containing sensitive content." Simply check this box if you see nuances of sexual innuendos and other things of that nature in your future.[3]

4.) The Photo has been Posted. Now what?

Looks like those drunken pictures of you from last weekend did in fact make their way onto Facebook and Twitter. Where do you go from here? After initially begging your friend to have mercy on your soul and delete the pictures, the next stop would be to visit either to Facebook Help Center or the Twitter Help Center for more information. Whether you wish to report the not-so-flattering pictures to your friend or to the site itself, both of the Help Centers above will help you in the process. Here's how.

Reporting the Photo on Facebook

The Facebook Help Center is composed of seven overarching themes; one of them entitled "Report Abuse or Policy Violations." Within this tab, one can find information about securing a hacked account and more in-depth privacy concerns. Also under this tab is a section entitled "Report a Violation" that gives virtually all information needed to handle any sort of site-based photo problem.

Although it may sound harsh, sometimes reporting an inappropriate Facebook photo is the most effective way of getting it off of the site forever. The reporting process is simple and only takes a second. If you feel that a Facebook photo is inappropriate and in need of reporting, locate the symbol at the top right corner of the photo and choose the "Report this Photo" option. Reporting a photo does not guarantee that Facebook will automatically remove it, for strict variations between the mass amount of people and cultures makes it quite difficult to determine what is even inappropriate. And finally, to answer the question everyone's wondering about – *no, people responsible for the photos you have reported do not see who reported them.*[4]

Reporting the Photo on Twitter

As I mentioned previously, pictures are way less popular on Twitter as they are on Facebook. Therefore, uncovering this site's policies about photo abuse was not nearly as simple. However, I did find that inappropriate content can be reported on this growing social media site, as well. For situations involving incriminating photos, a user can click the "Flag this media" button to the bottom right of the picture.

Aside from simply "flagging" the picture, a person can report highly inappropriate photos through the process of filing a support ticket. This support ticket can be found in the Twitter Help Center under the "Reporting Violations" section. This section has eight sub-ions within it, one of them called "How to Report Violations." Clicking this link will take you to a page full of various issues that can be reported on, one of them most notably being pornography. As Twitter in no way tolerates pornography, images akin to this type can be reported by filing a support ticket. A support ticket is sent directly to the Twitter Support team where they will decide how to handle the inappropriate picture. Again, filing a support ticket does not guarantee that the photo will be removed from the site.[5]

5.) Site-Related Consequences for Inappropriate Photos

Neither Facebook nor Twitter tolerates photos that would not be acceptable according to most people's standards. What happens when a picture of this nature pops up on these social media sites, though? Are there any site-related consequences? It just so happens that both Facebook and Twitter threaten removal from the sites altogether if dirty photos are discovered within your personal site. Moreover, serious instances of incriminating photos can lead to legal ramifications, as well, like jail time.

6.) What Inappropriate Pictures Can Lead to

While posting nude or intoxicated-beyond-belief photos of yourself sounds harmless, countless examples of successful people losing jobs and relationships over these kinds of pictures are all over the internet. The following stories were uncovered through a simple internet search. Sad as they are, they are completely true and should serve as a constant reminder of what posting questionable photos onto social media can do to one's relationships, career, and life in general.

A Cheerleader's Dream Turned Nightmare

18-year-old Caitlin Davis became the youngest pro-football cheerleader of all time. Things were going more than perfect until Davis engaged in some underage drinking and posed provocatively with her friends at a party. Her upper body was covered with magic marker that spelled out anti-Semitic remarks and references to male genitalia. Not surprisingly, the photos of the college student eventually made their way to Facebook where members of the New England Patriots staff saw them and immediately relieved Caitlin Davis of her cheerleading duties.[6]

A School Aide Convicted of Drinking Charge

Mary Ellen Hause worked part-time as a teacher's aide at Springboro High School near Dayton, Ohio. A picture of her and three of her students engaging in what appeared as underage alcohol consumption surfaced on Facebook in early 2009. The school's resource officer, Sgt. Don Wilson, discovered the photo while poking around a few of his students' Facebook accounts. Upon finding the photo of both Hause and the three underage girls with Smirnoff bottles in-hand, Wilson turned it over to the local police. She was eventually sentenced to 30 days in jail, a $500 fine, 10 days of trash pick-up, and three years of probation prohibiting her from consuming alcohol or having it in her house. As you probably guessed, she lost her job, too.[7]

Facebook Reveals Bigamist

Richard Barton, Jr., of Grand Rapids, Michigan, broke ties with his wife, Adina Quarto, after several years of marriage. Although Barton and Quarto had no communication for many years, they were still technically married and jointly caring for their six-year-old son. Barton unfriended Quarto on Facebook, a natural step in the letting-go process. However, Barton failed to adjust the privacy settings that would prohibit his wife from seeing his personal information, like photos. Quarto saw pictures of her husband (yes, husband) marrying another woman on a beach in early 2011, making him legally married to not one, but two women at the same time. Quarto called the police and Barton was arrested for bigamy.[8]

7.) One More Paragraph...

Before you read on, let's sum it all up. In a nutshell, this chapter has covered personal and site-related consequences for incriminating photos within social media, ways to prevent them from ending up on the sites, what can be done for these pictures' hopeful removal from Facebook or Twitter, and some real-life situations involving incriminating photos. I hope that what I have presented in this chapter has expanded your knowledge of incriminating photos on social media sites. Moreover, I encourage readers to heed my advice and listen to what this chapter says – my words may be the only thing between you and a very incriminating photo situation.

REFERENCES

1. "Incriminate." http://dictionary.reference.com/browse/incriminate. (Accessed February 29, 2012).
2. Facebook. "Approving and Removing Tags." Facebook Help Center. http://www. facebook.com/help/privacy/photos/approving-and-removing-tags. (Accessed February 29, 2012).
3. Twitter. "Media Settings and Best Practices." Twitter Help Center. https://support. twitter.com/articles/20169200. (Accessed February 29, 2012).
4. Facebook. "Tools for Addressing Abuse." Facebook Help Center. http://www.facebook.com/help/?faq=203081409728705&in_context. (Accessed February 28, 2012).
5. Twitter. "How to Report Violations." Twitter Help Center. https://support.twitter. com/groups/33-report-a-violation/topics/122-reporting-violations/articles/15789-how-to-report-violations.(Accessed February 29, 2012).
6. Chris Chase. "Patriots Cheerleader Booted due to Facebook Pictures." Yahoo! Sports. Last modified November 5, 2008. http://sports.yahoo.com/nfl/blog/shutdown_corner/post/Patriots-cheerleader-booted-due-to-incriminating?urn=nfl-119945.
7. Declan McCullagh. "Facebook Photo Convicts School Aide of Drinking Charge." CNet News. Last modified March 17, 2009. http://news.cnet.com/8301-13578_3-10197908-38.html.
8. Jolie O'Dell. "Facebook Photos Help to Incriminate Bigamist." Mashable. Last modified March 19, 2011. http://mashable.com/2011/03/19/facebook-photos-bigamy/.
9. "Drunk Girl Chugging Booze." Fugly. http://www.fugly.com/pictures/13490/drunk-sloot-chugging-booze.html. (Accessed February 28, 2012).
10. "An Open Letter to the Girl at the Party" College Candy. Last modified April 18, 2009. http://collegecandy.com/tag/too-drunk/.

CHAPTER 9

Lucy DeFruscio– "Cyber-bullying: Packs a Different Punch"

1. What is cyber-bullying?

2. What are the 6 signs to look for if someone is getting Cyber-bullied?

3. Can schools punish students who cyber-bully at home?

S ocial media is an important aspect of our everyday lives, but sometimes it can be a dangerous tool for young adults. Cyber-bullying is one of the means teenagers are using today to attack other teenagers. But what exactly is cyber-bullying? Well, according to the Olweus Bullying Prevention Program, bullying through email, instant messaging, chat room exchanges, web site posts, or digital messages or images sent to a cell phone or personal digital assistant (PDA) constitutes cyber-bullying.[1] It is most common among young people, but when an adult is involved, it may meet the definition of cyber-harassment or cyber-stalking, a crime that can have legal consequences and involve jail time.[2] Society has rid itself of the fights in the back alley after school and replaced them by going home and virtually attacking someone all night long. In a nut shell, it is a 24 hour, 7 days a week opportunity to verbally attack someone at school then go home and continue on social media sites such as Facebook and Twitter. Within this chapter, I will discuss personal stories from students who are victims of this danger, how parents can detect cyber-bullying in their home, the characteristics and consequences of the person who participates in the act, personal opinions from parents, and an organization to stop cyber-bullying.

Cyber-bullying happens all over the world. In West Virginia, some-one I will call Anonymous was cyber-bullied by a co-worker's wife for over a year. Anonymous was eighteen years old at the time when the cyber-bullying began. She never had a relationship with her co-worker, but they did engage in harmless flirting and a few kisses. There was never anything serious between them, and she never even met him outside of the workplace. Anonymous did not think it was fair to her co-worker's wife and called it off with him, choosing to apologize to his wife. His wife did not find this apology acceptable. For the next year, she cyber-bullied Anonymous constantly.

Not only did Anonymous receive multiple hateful and demeaning messages from the man's wife, but her social media accounts were also hacked. Also, accounts were created as impersonations of Anonymous and even her close friend's accounts were hacked. There were many accusations and harassments involved with this case, and these harassments occurred on many different social media tools. The tools used to cyber-bully included: MySpace, AOL Instant Messenger (AIM), email, text messaging, Twitter, Facebook, Skype, Wee World, Form Spring, and Zoosk.

From my interview with Anonymous, she noted at least fifty-eight accounts of cyber-bullying on all of the different social media tools men-tioned above. She was in a constant battle with a woman she did not even know over an affair that never even happened. The majority of the harassment accounts involve the wife threatening to beat Anonymous up, calling her demeaning names, and hacking into her accounts on Twitter, MySpace and Facebook making it so that Anonymous could not access them. A specific example that took the harassment to a new level was when the wife made a fake dating profile for Anonymous. Anonymous explained, "After receiving a text concerning 'Zoosk', I looked online at www.zoosk.com and found a dating profile of myself which had several pictures of me along with descriptions of myself that were taken from my Facebook or made up. I had never even heard of Zoosk before I received the message and I am not the one who made this account."

The correct assumption would be that Anonymous went to the police who did all they could to find the cyber-bullying wife and had a restraining order and other consequences for harassment put against her. Nope. Three years later, the police still have not called Anonymous back with any further news about her case. Anonymous' explanation of her police difficulties by explaining, "I went to the State Police Department order to try to get my accounts back and to request some sort of restraining order against the wife and her husband. I spoke with a Corporal there, and he instructed me to come back at a later date to have my laptop inspected by a computer tech that would then be able to discover the identity of the person hacking my account." Anonymous has yet to hear from the State Police.

After three years, the harassment has finally stopped. The best thing Anonymous did was that she never gave the wife a response or retaliated in a way that could further jeopardize her own safety. Anonymous' only defense was by saying, "Aside from once, right after my accounts were hacked, I had not sent her any messages that were not a reply to a message she had sent me first. During my conversation with the wife, I never threatened her safety, her family, or anything involving her. I told her that I would refuse to fight her and continually asked her to leave me alone." Anonymous hopes justice will one day be served to the wife because, according to state policies, cyber-bullying is a serious offense in West Virginia. For now, she waits and hopes for that day.

Another example of cyber-bullying involved a Wheeling Jesuit University student named Chris Bohinski. Bohinski was a victim of this type of bullying last year during a student-council election. He was running for Student Body President and had a vision of bringing recording artist Lady Gaga to WJU. For those of you who do not know, Lady Gaga has relatives who reside in Wheeling. Bohinski's slogan that he wrote in chalk on the WJU campus sidewalks stated, "Help Bring Lady Gaga to WJU, Vote for Chris and Brady." This slogan caused the cyber-bullying via Facebook.

The following morning, Bohinski was in Calculus class and received a text, which warned him not to log into Facebook because there were a number of rude statuses posted regarding Bohinski's goal of getting Lady Gaga to come to WJU. Bohinski explained, "I've never logged into Facebook and saw the entire newsfeed all about one person, and that one person was me. The first twenty statuses were all about me and my "promise" of bringing Lady Gaga to school for a concert that would cost $900,000."

Bohinski was in shock over this outbreak because this situation was blown out of proportion, and he had never made any definite promises regarding Lady Gaga's appearance at WJU. Bohinski is a very ambitious person who was not attempting to make promises that he could not keep. He wanted to show the student body his hard work and ambitious goals. In regards to the rude statuses posted about him, Bohinski never responded. "I didn't make any counter posts," Bohinski said. "I didn't make any statuses. I definitely read them all and shared them with my family." To Bohinski's knowledge, none of the students ever got in trouble for their bullying. "Current student government holders and students running against me even commented on the Facebook posts," Bohinski stated. Bohinski was upset to see student government officers make those statements because they were students who had visions just like he did; yet they were not sticking up for him.

Today, Bohinski will randomly see or hear about students discussing this situation. For instance, on Twitter, Bohinski read a tweet that said, "If you think we are going to win this game today, you probably think Lady Gaga is coming here too." Once cyber-bullying happens, it never really goes away. The severity level decreases over time, but people usually do not forget about it once it has happened. It is something that a person will carry around for the rest of his or her life.

People did not simply make negative remarks about Bohinski; he also had supporters who stood up for him in reaction to the cyber-bullying. "For every person that was mean, there was another person who was nice," Bohinski said. "If they heard someone talking about it, they would tell them Lady Gaga is from Wheeling." It was important to have support because it meant that Bohinski was not alone during this hard time. Supporting a victim of cyber-bullying is a positive contribution a person can give because the victim will not feel as bad knowing that someone else is there for him or her.

Cyber-bullying may be a hard thing to detect in your home because most teenagers are too afraid of telling any adults, such as parents, teachers, counselors, and administrators. According to Kids Health, there are six signs to look for if a parent thinks their child may be a victim of cyber-bullying. These six signs include: emotional distress during or after using the Internet or the phone, being very protective or secretive of digital life, withdrawal from friends and activities, avoidance of school or group gatherings, slipping grades, "acting out" in anger at home, and changes in mood, behavior, sleep, or appetite.[3] Parents should take these signs seriously because there are different levels of cyber-bullying. If a parent allows the situation to escalate without intervening, it could lead to a major situation, which could end up harming his or her child. All severities of cyber-bullying need to be addressed because a child's desire to fit in at school can mean the world to them and if it is not happening, a child could act out irrationally.

On the other side, the person who is the bully has certain characteristics that suggest participating in a specific form of cyber-bullying. According to the Olweus Bullying Prevention Program, these five characteristics include: anonymity, accessibility, punitive fears, bystanders, and disinhibition. Anonymity is a characteristic because it is easy to keep an identity hidden when a bully is harassing a victim over a computer compared to in person. Accessibility is also specific to cyber-bullying because, unlike regular bullying, cyber-bullying can happen at any time of the day and anywhere a bully has access to a computer. There are two main fears that occur for the victim, including both the fear of retribution from tormentors and fear that parents will remove computer or phone privileges. Bystanders are very different since cyber-bullying occurs via the Internet. Usually, they are a few people watching or assisting in playground bullying, while in cyber-bullying, if the bullying is posted on a popular social media site, there can be millions of bystanders who see it. Cyber-bullying makes bullying more available for large groups to see. The last characteristic, disinhibition, helps a bully have the courage to bully another person. With anonymity, a bully feels more encouraged to engage in the act because he or she feels like nobody knows who he or she is.[4]

These five simple characteristics can have a major effect on a bully's life, not to mention the victim's life. In general, bullying is something that is frowned upon in schools and has different levels of consequences based on the severity, school, and the grade level at which it occurs. The question parents have is if punishment for cyber-bullying is acceptable to be taken in the hands of the school system if it may or may not occur at school? According to the research article titled, "Extending the School Grounds – Bullying Experiences in Cyberspace?," cyberspace may not function as a separate risky environment but rather as an extension of the school grounds. This article states that "the 85% overlap between online and in-school bullying experiences and the 7-fold higher risk of online incidents among repeatedly targeted youth at school suggest that cyberspace is not a separate risk environment. Rather, cyberspace seems to be used as a forum that extends the school grounds."[5] The communication tools used to cyber-bully do not increase chances of bullying; they just give bullies an advantage to have more tools to get in contact with a person.

If cyberspace is an extension of school grounds, how do administrators enforce that cyber-bullying is unacceptable and considered in school bullying? Well, they treat each level of bullying in the same manner. In some cases, the victim goes as far as committing suicide. If this happens, punishment in a school will be major for the bully, and then the police deal with it from there if necessary. Schools can do what they want for punishment, but "harassing someone over the Internet subjects the bully to a misdemeanor, punishable by a fine of up to 500 dollars and 90 days in jail."[6] Essentially, most schools do deal with punishing students who are involved in cyber-bullying crimes. If these instances are severe enough, for instance, if death is involved, then the police will get involved and provide additional punishments.

There are instances in which a parent may think bullying toughens a child's skin or is not really severe because everyone gets "teased" sometimes. This judgment is unacceptable because a parent may not understand the entire situation or not know how severe bullying may be for his or her child. For instance, Megan Meier, a thirteen-year-old girl from Columbia, Missouri, committed suicide after being embarrassed by a fake online relationship with a boy named "Josh Evans." Meier's mom speaks out for her today to try and convince parents that cyber-bullying, or any type of bullying for that matter, is something to keep an eye on. During her presentation, Meier's mom states, "we have to change the environment of the way we look at a child who comes in to talk to us about if they're witnessing something. We need to make sure we keep empowering these bystanders because it's the only way we're going to win this war."[7]

This is a personal opinion about cyber-bullying from a first-hand account that has turned into a presentation for parents across the country to hear and see how serious this bullying is. This is a mom who did not have to do research in order to convince parents that cyber-bullying is a serious harm to a child's life. Rather, she lived it. "If we can get to one child at the end of the day that we can save, it's all worth it," Meier insisted.[7]

While parents can report cyber-bullying crimes to the police, they may get no response like the Anonymous case at the beginning of the chapter. Luckily, there are prevention organizations for victims that are great tools to help them overcome the emotions of being bullied. For example, the National Organization of Victim Assistance (NOVA) is an organization that has the mission "to champion dignity and compassion for victims of crime & crisis." NOVA is the oldest national victim organization in the United States and has four main values. According to the NOVA official website, these values and explanations include: "Compassion: We care about and respond to the plight of people and one another, accountability: Excellence in our work and justice in our cause means we honor our commitments, collaboration: Teamwork at every level is crucial to the work we do; passion: We are driven by the hope that what we do makes a difference."[8]

NOVA is just one of the many organizations available for parents of victims of cyber-bullying to use in order to gain access and help in dealing with this issue. NOVA provides information on how to deal with a victim of bullying, his or her rights, and resources to use in order to find out what to do if a parent wants the law involved. NOVA is here to help parents and victims receive the right treatment to ease the pain for a child. As stated previously, cyber-bullying can cause victims to do irrational things. Organizations like NOVA are essential to helping victims realize that they are not alone and that there is a way out and a better solution than suicide.[9]

As you can see, cyber-bullying is not something that should be taken lightly when a parent, teacher, administrator, or peer thinks a teenager might be a victim. Cyber-bullying, like any other type of bullying, can force a teenager to do something irrational such as commit suicide because he or she may feel like it is the only way to stop the pain. Parents need to talk to their kids to let them know that they are there for them and that help is available. The help available can as extreme as a psychiatric help or as simple as a guidance school counselor. No matter how severe, someone is always available to help a teenager get past bullying in order to start living his or her life again. A parent's care can mean all the difference in the world for a child who needs love and kindness more than anything.

REFERENCES

1. "What is Cyber-bullying?," *Olweus Bullying Prevention Program*, n.d., http://www.violencepreventionworks.org/public/cyber_bullying.page, and (17 April 2012).

2. "Cyberbullying," *Kids Health*, January 2012, http://kidshealth.org/parent/positive/talk/cyberbullying.html, and (14 February 2012).

3. "Cyberbullying," *Kids Health*, January 2012, http://kidshealth.org/parent/positive/talk/cyberbullying.html, and (14 February 2012).

4. "What is Cyber-bullying?," *Olweus Bullying Prevention Program*, n.d., http://www.violencepreventionworks.org/public/cyber_bullying.page, and (17 April 2012).

5. Jaana Juvonen and Elisheva F. Gross, "Extendng the School Grounds? – Bullying Experiences in Cyberspace," *Journal of School Health* (2008): 496-505, accessed (14 March 2012).

6. Millie A. Cavanaugh, "Cyberbullying Can Have Deadly Consequences," *Aspen Education Group*, n.d., http://www.aspeneducation.com/Article-cyberbulling-consequences.html, and (14 February 2012).

7. Kate Moritz, "Mother of cyberbullying victim speaks to students, parents," *Missourian*, n.d., http://www.columbiamissourian.com/stories/2011/02/09/mother-cyber-bullying-victim-speaks-rock-bridge-parents/, and (14 February 2012).

8. "NOVA Overview," *National Organization of Victim Assistance*, n.d., http://www.trynova.org/overview, and (14 March 2012).

9. *National Organization of Victim Assistance*, n.d., http://www.trynova.org/, and (14 March 2012).

CHAPTER 10

Sam Bauman– "It's Complicated"

1. What are the 4 steps to Facebook flirting?

2. What is a "poke"?

3. What are 2 of the don'ts of Social media?

In the all too often roller coaster ride we call relationships there are many unique and unfathomable reasons why some work and some just don't. One of the most prominent of these reasons that seems to factor into relationship success or failure can be a direct result of communication, or lack thereof. Of course being a communication major I myself am I bit biased, but nonetheless, most strong relationships seem to have a strong sense of communication between the two people involved. What happens, however, when this relationship is brought to the next level of commitment? When the whole world can see, judge and constantly check up on the "status" of your relationships. That moment when you as a couple decide to make your relationship..... Facebook Official! Now before we go any further I'll back track a step or two and explain just exactly how one goes about changing their relationship status via Facebook, and what each of these confusing choices means.

Alright, so for you Facebook newbie's out there I'll try and be as detailed as possible in helping you locate and edit your relationship status. Once logging onto Facebook you will want to go to your own profile which can be accessed by clicking on your name in the top right corner of the page. After arriving on your profile you will next locate the "About Me" section, usually found in the upper left near your profile picture. Clicking on this will direct you to another page where it lists, well, all about you. You next want to scroll down until you find the section titled "Basic Info." There will be an option in the top right of this section that says "edit." Click it. A window will then appear. In that window is a section labeled "Relationship Status," if you have not changed it already it most likely reads "Single." To change this click the box, this causes a list of options to appear. For the most part the options are self explanatory (in a relationship, single, married, engaged, widowed, divorced, etc.). However, you might come across a few that just darn right confuse you; most common of these being "It's Complicated." "It's Complicated" can really mean a few different things depending on the person and relationship. This is generally selected either towards the end of a relationship or during the very beginning; it was intended to give notice that you're trying to work out the fine details of the relationship with whomever "It's Complicated" with. However, it has come more recently to be interpreted as, "well I'm kinda sorta with someone occasionally when things are good and stuff but like if something better comes along or whatever like its cool, we're like on a break sorta." If that confused you, well then you're right on track. In reality, if "It's Complicated," it's really "not happening," I digress.

After carefully selecting your new and improved relationship status, Facebook will so kindly ask whom you are entering a Facebook official relationship with. At this point, you can choose to either leave it blank or type in the name of your significant other, at which point a notification will be sent to that person to be accepted or denied. When accepted (hopefully), your profile page will now include what type of relationship you're in, and with who you are in it, and just like that you're now... Facebook Official!

Unfortunately, becoming Facebook Official doesn't just happen overnight. As with any relationship, it takes time to build up to it. Within any social environment with members of the opposite sex, flirting of some sort will most likely ensue, and that goes the same for Facebook. Unlike common flirting approaches, flirting on Facebook takes special skills in communicating without actually communicating. To attempt the Facebook flirt is a bold move only suggested to the most confident and socially inept people. It requires delicate awareness of the online world and a keen persistence balancing flawlessly on the fine line between cute and creeper. There are four crucial steps that should be followed for all Facebook flirts.

Not included in these steps of course is the ever important "friend request." Without this, all Facebook flirtery would be impossible. After the acceptance of the friend request you want to move in slowly; don't rush into anything; let the recently requested friend have time to get used to seeing your occasional status popping up on their newsfeed. Once you feel they've had time to have profile recognition of you in the Facebook world wait for the opportune status of theirs to show up on your own timeline. The last thing you want to do here is force "the like," so when the appropriate status comes across, maybe something generic like "what a supertastic day," make "the like" leap and go ahead and like that status. Now give it time to mellow; maybe a few more status likes throughout the week so the preliminary interest is now evident. From here you have now established a regularity of interactions which opens the door to "the like" big leagues with the added "likability" of pictures. This is where the fine line of cute to creep can become dangerously fine, by liking one too many pictures or the wrong type of picture, you can go from potential Facebook flirt buddy to the ever feared "unfriended."

"The Poke"

With careful and smooth liking skills now added to your Facebook flirting repertoire your ready to move onto an even more controversial move, "the poke." The poke has been an evolving flirt technique since Facebook's early days. Seemingly more subtle than "the like," "the poke" is a more private approach to Facebook flirting. Only visible on the homepage of the intended pokey, the poker can be confident knowing that even if this approach is unsuccessful it will be kept between pokey and poker (well, as much as anything is kept secret these days). While the added secrecy can help one save face from possible public rejection, it is one of the bigger Facebook flirt steps to be made because it is such an individualized approach. Unlike "the like," this is a one on one flirt technique with just your name on the line; a denied repoke can prove detrimental. "The poke," if used correctly, can take you to the next level of Facebook flirtitude, but used in the wrong context or without establishing "the like" first can set you back and put you on the fast track to creeperville.

"The Comment"

The third step in this highly evolved social media structured flirting is known simply as "the comment." This move is not to be done without first having accomplished "the like," but can often be switched in order with "the poke." A premature comment can lead you down a dangerous path, not to mention put you at risk of public humiliation if "the comment" is left uncommented on. In comparison to "the poke," "the comment" is only to be used after you are positive. A return comment will take place, a comment left sitting empty on a profile is a sure way to knock yourself out of contention with a potential Facebook flirtation. Of course a comment can be used in a variety of venues, posted on a wall, a picture, or a status. The content of each of these should be carefully considered before making any sort of comment-ment. A smoothly worded and placed comment can be just the thing to take your Facebook flirting to the final plateau.

"That Chat"

The height of Facebook flirting is when communication is at its highest during..... "the chat." Chatting on Facebook is the AIM of the current day; it gives you the ability to keep a constant conversation with someone, similar to texting, but at a more consistent pace. This is your chance to really let your personality shine. If you've gotten to this point you must have mastered the first three steps, so when moving on to the fourth one, just keep doing what you're doing. Jumping into chatting too soon can prove awkward and eliminate any future chat possibilities, so be sure you have established a steady stream of commenting (both ways) before moving on to any chat like activities. Once chat has been established play it cool. If they don't respond at any point within the chat, let it slide; the last thing you want to do is send multiple messages in a row without response. Nothing says Facebook flirt desperate like a one way chat conversation. After a few quality chat sessions with the occasional flirtatious lines used here and there it's only a matter of time before real world conversation will take place. With the combined use of all four of these Facebook flirt steps, used correctly and in the right order, you'll be on your way to Facebook official in no time.

After smoothly maneuvering your way through the challenging trials of flirting on Facebook, you might have made the leap to Facebook Official. Now you may be thinking that you're in the clear, and that you've jumped the biggest hurdle when it comes to relationships on Facebook. It is quite the opposite, however; being in a relationship, especially one that is public on Facebook, is a whole new battle in itself. Similar to flirting on Facebook, being in a relationship on Facebook can walk a fine line, between crazy and cute. Just like handling a relationship in other social settings you want to find a happy medium between seeming uninterested and being all over each other. When it comes to the relationship on Facebook, there are a few general do's and don'ts.

Do's
1. Make it visible on your profile
2. Occasionally be in each other's profile picture
3. Make it a point when celebrating birthdays or anniversaries (length of 1yr or more)
4. Post the occasional funny video or joke on their wall (once to twice a week max)

Don'ts
1. Share a Profile
2. Post mushy comments on a regular basis
3. Post "I love you" less than six months into relationship
4. Have the same profile picture

Now that you have a brief idea on the taboo's of Facebook relationships we'll dive deeper into some of the nitty gritty when it comes to playing it cool. One of the biggest issues that couples come across in Facebook relationships is jealousy. Here are a few things to keep in mind

They don't have a crush on them...
1. Just because they post on someone of the opposite sex's wall
2. Just because they're in a picture with them

3. Just because they like their status

4. Just because they friend requested them

By keeping these four simple thoughts in mind you can avoid a handful of pointless fights. If it really is bothering you, try communicating with them instead of pouting and trying to get even with them through Facebook. I will go more in depth on this subject later in the chapter. Going hand in hand with jealousy is sharing a Facebook password with your significant other. This is a tough decision to make but can make or break a relationship. On one hand, if you don't tell them your password they might think you have something to hide. On the other hand, if something does go wrong and they have access to your profile, they can do as much as unfriending people to posting something that could get you in trouble. I will say when it comes to passwords don't ask for theirs, if they want to give it to you they will. Until then, it's a question better left unasked. Managing your relationship without Facebook is hard enough, and adding in the grueling pressures of social media just makes it harder. Without proper social awareness it can take your relationship down a scary path and eventually lead towards the Facebook Fallout.

Facebook Fallout

Facebook Fallout can happen to the strongest of couples and can sprout up at anytime. This occurs when jealousy is at its peak. When a poke, a like, or a seemingly too friendly comment starts getting under your skin, you can be sure a fallout is soon to follow. With the fallout, inevitable a break up is just around the corner. Now a breakup is hard enough in the "real world," but a Facebook breakup can be a whole new ball game for many former Facebook official couples. Going from "In a relationship" to "single" is a tender situation for both of the newly found Facebook singles, and made that much harder knowing your failed relationship is now public news on the newsfeeds of all your Facebook friends. This can be scary new territory for many people and is generally handled in one of four ways.

1. Deleting

Deleting is, well, quite self explanatory really. This is when one, or both, of the former Facebook relationship members decides that for one reason or another they should delete their former boyfriend/

girlfriend on Facebook. Most will tell you it's because they are too tempted to see what their ex is up to these days and it only makes them miss them more. Some will tell you it's because they can't stand the thought of knowing they may be moving on to a new Facebook flirt. Even more likely than the two previous is that they know a delete of an ex will surely frustrate them and they see it as a way to get a final little jab in. Now, in reality, it is most likely a combination of these three reasons. As for its effectiveness, although it may help you to "miss them less," it doesn't delete them out of your life, just off your timeline.

2. Quoting

Quoting is a technique most commonly used by the more sensitive types. This entails the use of inspirational or motivational quotes as daily status, either with the intention of truly motivating one's self or showing your ex and the rest of the Facebook world you're doing just fine as a single. Some of the more common quotes are ones dealing with how the single life is better, or you don't need anyone else, or something about how being knocked down can't keep you down, blah blah blah basically just a public way to get attention without begging for it. Overall, quoting is probably a better choice than deleting, but still a very attention grabbing approach and might just show how much you really are hurt.

3. The Jealousy Card

The jealousy card is a bolder and quite selfish approach that is sadly used more often than not. This is when one or both of the involved takes it upon themselves to Facebook flirt it up with anyone possible. Whether that means posting photos, tagging, commenting, and downright status dedicating to another potential girlfriend/ boyfriend, the intent is to create jealousy in their ex. The biggest flaw in this, other than being just not very nice at all, is that it can often backfire in the midst of getting back what they're dishing out, or leading to the "delete," which would make such flirting pointless. If you couldn't tell, this approach is both a bold and commonly ineffective one. All it does is show the Facebook community either you didn't care, or you still do.

4. Playing it Cool

Playing it cool. Well it says right there "cool." Now that's something everyone wants to be in real life and that is just as true on Facebook. I have found that the best approach in this unfortunate situation is to do just that, play it cool. Maybe keep away from Facebook for a week or two, give it time to blow over before making any moves in the online world. The old saying "don't make any decisions out of anger" comes to mind. If you jump to an angry status, perhaps a premature delete, or a hurtful jealousy card move you may just worsen an already poor situation. Give it time, collect your thoughts, and when you finally make the leap to log back on just keep it classy. Like some friends' statusses, post about your family, and keep your business your business and off social media. That my friends is playing it cool and handling the Facebook Fallout in a "like"able way.

What Can We Learn?

Well it's been a long chapter. I may have "poked" some unpleasant buttons, maybe "commented" on a topic to close to home, heck maybe you didn't even "like" it but there are a few keys things you can take away from this. For starters, leave online dating to online dating sites. Facebook is for friends, no one wants to see your relationship step by step on a timeline, and no one should want that to be seen. Keep it private. If your brother's piano teacher's daughter's cousin can tell you who you're dating and how things are going you've got a problem, save the details for your real friends not the Facebook kind. Communication is crucial. I'm talking real life face to face words coming out of your mouth listening type of communication, not clever typed out tagged posted and liked type communication. If you can't talk to them in person there's a problem. Communication is key in any relationship; without it you're just two quiet individuals. Finally, play it cool. Don't post out of anger or in extreme happiness. Give it a second to sink in before making any bold moves. Heck, it's not like Facebook is going anywhere, but a poorly phrased post can stick with you forever. Don't let P.P. (poor posting) happen to you. Relationships are great whether they're "Facebook Official" or not, and in the end it's about the memories you make not the comments you "like." See I guess it's not so complicated after all.

CHAPTER 11

Megan Truelove – "Finding the Right Key"

1. Where is the best place to look for upcoming music or bands?

2. Pandora finds music for you using what technology?

3. Why do artists turn to social media?

People know him as West Virginia's Ponce De'Leioun. He grew up in Wheeling, West Virginia and currently attends Fairmont State University. Starting out as a mixture artist, he has recently been shooting music videos as an unsigned artist in what he refers to as his "create a buzz stage." I was able to contact Ponce to talk to him about his personal music career and the huge role that social networking sites have played in helping him communicate with and broaden his audience.

When accessing his personal website, it is clear he's not an amateur to the music business. The site, which is currently managed by a web manager, has a web design and layout that are user-friendly. According to Ponce, "The site is simple, yet very professional."

MySpace was the first form of social networking used to showcase Ponce's music when he was in high school. Ponce adds, "It made it very easy for people [to] stay in tune with my music and updates." He now makes use of several sites, including Facebook, Twitter, and hotnewhiphop. YouTube is the site Ponce plans on using more than all the others this year with the hope of attracting even more attention to his page through updating his account with new music and performance videos. Ponce is so confident in YouTube that when I asked him why he would choose YouTube over all the rest he responded, "...for the simple reason... Just about anything you upload has a chance of going viral depending on what push you give it. Once I upload a video, it is easy for anybody in the world to come in contact with it."

As far as advice for those also attempting to succeed in the music industry, Ponce advises, "Don't give up. It's not an easy path to drive down. Yet, if you drive slowly you will have much more time to think and make smart decisions. It takes a lot of time and dedication, if you have that you will be fine. I'd also suggest learning the business aspects of music, not just wanting to rap or sing. The business aspect is what will make you outshine other artists."

Ponce was able to utilize social networking to build a "buzz" that has begun to open doors for him. Starting out, he didn't have the cash funding available forout of state performances and conventions. He is now being invited to receive opening spots for famous acts, being invited to shows, and being asked for collaboration requests. Through the use of social networking sites, Ponce De'Leioun has created a career without having to leave the state.[1]

The Sites – What do people use to listen to and find new music?

Now I'm no musical expert to say the least. So maybe you're thinking, what makes me qualified to share what I've learned about musical sites over the years with you. Here, in my opinion, is my qualification – like most of the world, I am a member of the audience, one of the people who supports others talents through listening, watching, and becoming a fan. As a fan, it is my job to obsess over my favorite new and old discoveries. That's where social networking helps me to live my job title out to its fullest potential, like all the other people who are living with the title of being members of the audience. My personal "go to" site is Pandora Radio. I've discovered so many new songs and artists by entering in the search box a certain artist or genre that I'm in the mood to hear. I have my "go to" stations on the site, but I also like experimenting with new ones. There are so many social networking sites available for the use of artists and their fans. However, having an account for every single site that is actually good can cause a headache. Starting out with quality instead of quantity is the key here. But which sites should people focus on? In our case, we will focus on three sites that have each seen their fair share of popular musicians - MySpace, YouTube, and Pandora. So let's begin the search!

MySpace

Lance Clark, a freshman at West Virginia University, uses MySpace as an easy way to listen to new music and learn updates about his favorite bands. MySpace allows its users to listen to free unlimited full length audio streaming from any band or artist on the site. Plus, MySpace involves more than just listening to music. It engages a variety of entertainment aspects from presentations, invitations to gigs, interactions with listeners, and promotions by fans. Anyone can put music onto MySpace. The site includes major, independent, and unsigned artists. All it takes is the time and effort of setting up the free profile. Editors choose featured artists. These artists are featured based on which ones are getting particular attention on the site from users and which artists are contributing new or interesting music.[2]

YouTube

Killeen Schlegel, a sophomore at Wheeling Jesuit University, says she uses YouTube because it has become a sort of reference site for our generation and the site can be used to look up "legit" music videos to her favorite songs. She also enjoys that the newest hits she hears on the radio can be viewed instantly, unlike many sites where listening is the only available option. YouTube allows for users to browse and search for a variety of different videos, which include both originally created videos and official music videos. YouTube is free and accessible to viewers with or without a YouTube account. However, those who actually wish to publish content must set up an account. Anyone can post videos to the site, which are then available to be viewed by anyone.

YouTube also offers a Partnership Program that allows revenue to be generated through original videos that are uploaded and shared on the site, while offering copyright protection to the user and offering design and feature upgrades. To qualify for the partnership, users must regularly submit original videos to the site that receive thousands of YouTube views. According to the YouTube Partner Agreement, artists have no guarantee of how much they will be paid, or if they will even be paid at all. Compensation is generated based off of advertising revenue when viewers access a video.[3]

Pandora

Michelle Pottratz, a sophomore at Wheeling Jesuit University, enjoys using Pandora to discover new artists and music that are not played on the radio. She often finds songs that she really enjoys and would have never heard had she not listened to a particular Pandora station. Pandora Radio is a free internet radio and recommendation service. Users create stations by entering an artist or song, and the Music Genome Project of the site continues to choose selections that are similar. For those of you who are unfamiliar with the Music Genome Project, to put it simply, it is the representation of a song by a list of attributes about the particular song corresponding to the characteristic of the music, allowing for similar songs to be grouped together. [4]

Exactly how is the music that is aired on the Pandora site chosen? Pandora's music is discovered through searching and watching blogs, radio stations, show listings, and charts. When artists reach a level of prominence, their music will most likely be played on this site. In other words, if you're an artist getting attention from an audience, you have a chance of being a part of the Pandora collection. But, being discovered by Pandora isn't the only way to appear on the site. Auditioning by a web based submission is a second option that involves some time and effort but could be worth it for many artists trying to reach a larger audience. [5]

The ads that appear on Pandora are used to help keep the music service streaming. Music royalty fees are used as compensation each time a song is aired on the site. The advertising allows the cost to be free to listeners while compensating the artists at the same time. Another option is upgrading by paying a $36 fee for the year, causing the short advertisements to be banished, and allowing for an unlimited number of skips from the listening experience while still paying the royalty fees.

What about the others?

There are so many social networking sites that involve entertainment, especially on the music side of things. Favorites will vary among users and it is obviously impossible to include all of the sites here. However, just to name a few more popular options that may not be as obvious as the previously named but are just as well put together, there are ReverbNation, Spotify, and Bandcamp.

Greg Mulley, a sophomore at West Virginia University, says he uses ReverbNation because it allows bands to host their music and gives them a URL that they can distribute to fans and post places to get new fans, which is a attractive feature for Mulley who is a member of local bands. ReverbNation is a music-marketing platform that provides artists, managers, record labels, and venues an interactive site to collaborate and communicate with one another, while also reaching out to an audience. On the other hand, Spotify, a downloadable music streaming site, allows its users to create playlists and share them with other users. Bandcamp serves as both an online music store and artist promotion site used mainly by independent artists.

Upcoming Stars?

Let's face it, when it comes to getting your name out into the world these days social networking can be your best friend. So take advantage of it! Don't be afraid to learn and experiment with using new sites as they continue to make appearances on the Internet at a rapid speed, showing no signs of slowing down. It is important to remember not get too carried away with trying to make an appearance on every site that is available. It's just not worth it. It is important to remember that the Internet, when used effectively can be a very significant tool in promoting music and connecting with fans.

So whether you're looking to find your present-day favorite artists, discover new artists, or promote your own talent, there are more than enough social networking sites to explore that should meet your every fancy! There's no need to stick to just the sites we've mentioned here though. Explore the World Wide Web and begin your search for finding the right key for you!

REFERENCES

1. Ponce De'Leioun, (hip hop artist from Wheeling, WV), interview by Megan Truelove, Email. March 26, 2012.
2. MySpace, "MySpace Music Facts Page." http://creative.myspace.com/au/marketing/musichub/local/musicFaqs.htm.
3. E-Junkie.Info, "All About YouTube Partnership Program." Last modified Feb. 22, 2011. http://www.e-junkie.info/2011/02/all-about-youtube-partnership-program.html.
4. Pandora, "About Pandora." http://www.pandora.com/about.
5. Michael, Zapruder. "Getting Your Music Into Pandora." *KnowTheMusicBiz. com,* Nov. 19, 2010. http://www.knowthemusicbiz.com/getting-your-music-into-pandora-by-michael-zapruder/.

CHAPTER 12

Katherine Fey– "Tweet Styles of the Rich and Famous"

1. Who has the most twitter followers on twitter?

2. How do I know if it is really a celebrity on twitter?

3. How do I find celebrities to follow that appeal to my interests?

Most of us as a population are immensely intrigued by the lifestyles of the rich and famous. Foremost of these rich and famous people of whom we are so highly infatuated by, are professional athletes. Since most of the pro athletes we see today have come from a normal way of life at one point, we seem to relate to them and they can give the general population hope that they can too one day achieve a similar stature.

Athletes have come into the age of social media along with the rest of society in full force if not by a greater magnitude. With the launch of twitter becoming so popular, pro athletes have used it as a tool to reach out to their fans. Facebook is also another form of social media in which these athletes connect with followers or "friends" in this case. From reaching out to their viewers to explain situations to making humorous commentary, Facebook and Twitter has become one of the top ways for fans to get to know their idols.

Who writes on their pages?

Most times, the public is not able to know if the athletes they think they are following are actually writing on their own sites or not. Sometimes it may change between who is the author on the sites, but we are finding that more and more today it is actually the true person expressing their actual thoughts and activities throughout the day. Ultimately only they and their publicist and managers will know who is behind the screen writing, but as a avid follower myself, I can say that it is nice to think that the athletes are actually taking the time to post to their fans.

There can be good, bad, and stupid sides to the actual athlete writing on their own wall or feed (twitter). A positive example would be that they are showing that they actually care about their followers and fans. Davonte Shannon always makes a point to tweet back at his followers when they mention him in a post for the most part, so long as he has the time to be able to do so. He thinks that this gives him more credibility with his fans. When athletes such as Shannon post on their own accounts it can often times make them more likeable to the public and give themselves a more down to earth quality.[3] All in all, normal people write on their own media outlets, so why shouldn't they? They also appear much more relatable when they are not allowing someone else speak on their behalf. Sometimes stories can get twisted when it comes to what the athlete views as right and what their manager deems as correct.

On the flip side, when a publicist or manager monitors an athlete's account, they can make sure at all times what is being said about the athlete and what their player is saying to the public. Often times, athletes say things in the spurt of the moment which get twisted. In order to illuminate this from happening some athletes are completely banned from social media or they are restricted by time of day or their managers and publicists run their entire pages. One loses credibility when they have their pages ran by someone who is not them. Managers always seem to have a hidden agenda when it comes to their players, therefore the credibility issue is key. Also, one can never be sure if they are being honest. Managers don't know what is going through their players mind at all times, therefore nobody can be certain other than the individual themselves whether the statements are accurate or not.

I have found through talking to the pro athletes themselves that the best way to run their sites is by having a mix between them and their managers having access to the statements being sent out to the public. It allows for accurate and intelligent statements to be sent out, but viewers know that the facts are getting out to them. Nobody wants to be lied to, which is why credibility is so important to viewers.

Crisis management

Training on crisis management for professional athletes usually begins with a period of silence. This time of silence is simply to allow for the true story to reach the surface of the headlines. Once the truth is stated, there will be a public apology that follows. This apology will be pre-written by a team of specialists in crisis management. This would be the same in cases of high profiled colleges dealing with scandal, or the downfalls of a corporation. Close attention should be paid to the sincerity of the athletes during their apology, due to the simple fact that they are athletes...not actors.

Davonte Shannon speaks on this matter stating, "Many of my fellow teammates are awful liars, and we all get nervous when we get in front of a camera. Everyone would be able to tell if we were lying straight through our teeth."[4]

"Many courses are given to athletes in most Division 1 colleges because of their constant image in the public eye," Coach Jim Walker.[5] These courses outline procedures on how their should conduct themselves at all times, whether they are in season or not, in school or at home for the summer, and on the field or back at their campus. With the advice from all of their professors and coaches, the inevitable can happen should they make a poor decision.

As the viewers, we must decide whether we believe their stories on their social media pages. Soon after their public apology, we will be seeing postings by the athletes. Should we believe them, they will receive a large fan base, but if we do not take their apology as valid, they may be forced to go as far as to delete their pages.

Around the world, we are all fascinated by the lives of the rich and famous. With their constant exposure, one can only imagine how difficult it would be to be certain they were never making a mistake, as we all have at some point in life. As far as I can see, social media has allowed for the athletes and other celebrities to have a more personal advantage to getting their fans to be able to see what and who their true personality is to be. We should all embrace social media in this regard by allowing us to have means of constant communication with those we obsess over daily.

REFERENCES

1. Shannon, Davonte. Interview by Katherine Fey. Phone Interview. March 16, 2012.
2. Ibib "Shannon."
3. Ibib "Shannon."
4. Ibib "Shannon."
5. Walker, Jim. Interview by Katherine Fey. Wheeling Jesuit University. February 25, 2012.

CHAPTER 13

Kara DeSantis– "This Just In…"

1. What does the phrase "Google it" mean?

2. "Hoaxes on twitter remind us how easily false information can spread and that it is our responsibility to check it out."

   True or False

3. What is "Citizen Journalism"?

CNN, FOX News, and any other larger news station used to be popular ways of finding news. Before the internet and all of its wonders, people solely relied on television, radio and word of mouth. Though word of mouth is still a top source for receiving information, the internet is a close contender for number one. Think about any situation you have been in when someone told you about a breaking news story what was your next move to find out about what happened? Typically, people will turn to their smart phones, laptops or tablets and search for stories on the web. Google is one of the most popular search engines to date. "Google it" is now an acceptable phrase used to tell someone to search on Google. It is incredible how far we have come from using newspapers to asking Siri on the iPhone 4s to find information.

The saying "good news travels fast" is a fine slogan for news online. An even better statement would be that any news travels fast online. While reading this book you could tweet anything you desired and it would be out there for the world to see. What if it is something about another person? You have the right to say what you feel, but how far can or will it go?

When asked, five Wheeling Jesuit students agreed on their two most popular news sources being Twitter and Facebook. These two websites have changed the world of social media in a matter of a few short years. Anything you could think of can be posted on either site with a chance of the information being incorrect.

On Twitter, people are claimed to be dead every day, typically they are celebrities' Twitter pages being filled with trends of fatality. The hashtag #RIP has been used to spread rumors of false deaths such as: Chris Brown, Cher and even Mr. Bean. According to **Pamela Brown Rutledge**, Director of the **Media Psychology Research Center**,

> "Unfortunately for Twitter, part of the fallout is that these celebrity death hoaxes diminish the perception of Tweets as authentic sources of late-breaking information... In this case, the hoaxes remind us how easily false information can spread and that it is our responsibility to check it out." [1]

This brings up my next topic, how can we trust what is put on the web every day?

As previously stated, celebrities' false deaths are tweeted about every day. The fact that any person with a valid e-mail address possesses this power is mind boggling. Rumors spread quickly over the web and once it is tweeted, it may be re-tweeted forming a potential trend.

According to Dr. Brown Rutledge, the best advice before you believe everything you see on Twitter or Facebook would be, as stated, to do some research on the topic. If you read someone died, use the search engine online and find articles from reliable sources, don't believe a fifteen year old girl sitting in her bedroom with nothing better to do. Find the facts before you become a gullible addict on the web. This chapter is not to turn you away from believing online sources, it is merely a warning that every user online is not factual.

Coincidently, every respected news organization is not factual either. On January 2, 2006 a disaster occurred in southern West Virginia that made waves across the United States. A mine in Upshur County, West Virginia collapsed, trapping thirteen workers underground for two days. Numerous media sources broadcast news claiming that twelve of the thirteen trapped workers had survived, when in all actuality, there was one sole survivor.

The alleged news of the surviving twelve came about from a miscommunication between the rescue team and the command center. Between fifteen and twenty minutes had passed before they discovered the error. By that time, however, news had spread and families were already expressing happiness and relief.

The news of the survivors was reported on web sites such as CNN. com and news stations including the Associated Press and Reuters. It was a matter of hours before the news of survivors was reported as incorrect causing anarchy in the Sago Baptist Church, where the families of the miners waited impatiently. The family members were in an uproar, one man even attempted to attack a mine official over the misunderstanding.

Multiple news sources the next day had run false headlines and incorrect articles about the disaster. Even *The Pittsburgh Post-Gazette* had taken part in the fiasco by publishing a headline stating "Miracle at Sago: 12 Miners Alive". These media sources spent days apologizing to the families and friends of the deceased miners. This tragedy is a reminder to check the facts before believing everything you read.

When word of a story breaks out, it has the ability to spread like wild fire. Sometimes it reaches the public without ever being on the local news. This is all made possible by citizen journalism, which Bowman and Willis defined as, "the collection, dissemination, and analysis of news by the public, by means of cell phones, digital cameras, blogs, etc."[2] Citizen journalism is more prominent than ever, with blogs, Twitter and Facebook it is almost too easy to be a journalist.

The issue many people have with citizen journalism is the credibility each source offers. Blogs and posts on websites typically are very opinionated pieces of information people share to spread their thoughts or feelings about subjects. These opinions may be biased or inaccurate, but someone searching the web for information may not know that. This is one aspect that is important to watch out for.

One aspect of citizen journalism is posting podcasts or videos on YouTube or other similar websites. On YouTube, videos have the potential of effortlessly becoming viral in a matter of no time. Once enough people view the video, it can take off and reach the eyes of millions of people displaying the power of social media.

This power is not only a negative concept of social media, it can also have a positive side. Calling, texting, receiving alerts on cell phones and homepages of websites instantly update anyone with access to them about what is happening now. On January 24, 2011 I was sitting in my communications class awaiting my professor's arrival. She startled the class after she burst through the door telling everyone to YouTube a video of an airport bombing in Moscow. We all hurriedly typed it into YouTube's search engine and in no time were watching videos of a smoke filled airport with bodies scattered on the floor.

The entire class fell silent when our professor informed us that this bombing had happened only minutes ago. We were watching the first witness video from a suicide bombers attack on Moscow Domodedovo Airport. It did not take long for news stations to broadcast about the event, and when they did the YouTube video was aired on numerous stations.

Although we cannot trust everything that is posted online, we still heavily rely on social media to feed us information. It is our responsibility to seek out the truth behind the stories posted on social media sites. No matter what you think is right, always search for truth behind it. In the words of Albert Einstein, "A man should look for what is, and not for what he thinks should be."

REFERENCES

1. http://www.psychologytoday.com/blog/positively-media/201203/ rip-twitter-celebrity-death-hoaxes

2. Bowman, S. and Willis, C. "We Media: How Audiences are Shaping the Future of News and Information." 2003, *The Media Center at the American Press Institute..*

CHAPTER 14

Emily Amos – "Back to the Future"

1. What happened to Paige Duke the Nascar sprint cup girl?

2. Has anything like this ever happened on twitter?

3. How would you think Children's Miracle Network would use social media?

Did you ever think that one click of a mouse could change a person's life forever? Well, in today's technological world, more and more people are becoming present online. Whether it is through creating profiles on Facebook, or through creating account names on Twitter, the increase in social media over the last ten years has created many positive benefits and outcomes. However, lurking behind such benefits are the horror stories of social media that no one likes to address or talk about. Regardless of the stereotypical actions taken today, this chapter is going to address those cases as a reminder to always be careful of how you use your social media, especially in today's world where things can be retraceable and accessed at any time of the day. Also within this chapter, you will find stories pertaining to the ways social media is being used to change and save lives and is creating a web of opportunities no one ever imagined would surface.

How social media is used depends greatly on who is on the other side of the screen. Some may say it is a way of self-expression; others may claim they only use it to stay in touch. Regardless of what your purpose is on the web, it is how you use the materials at your fingertips that really matters. Once you type those few words or upload those few pictures and click "post" your life has drastically changed, whether you realize it or not. Through every post, like, or retweet you use, the World Wide Web can get an image of you, who you are, what your interests are, and even what you do for fun. There are some individuals and companies out there that use this capability to benefit others, and there are others that tend to abuse it. Social media should come with a huge caution button on every page, because a personal responsibility arises within each and every individual as soon as they access these sites for the first time. How people choose to use social media and the decisions they make along the way effect each person's present and will continue to affect their future.

In July 2011, a tragic event occurred over the web that caused a young woman to lose her job and in fact, crushed her dream. Paige Duke was one of three NASCAR Sprint Cup girls that had what some would claim to be the dream job. She was able to travel all over the United States to NASCAR races and events. As her story is publically known, nude pictures of Duke surfaced online in the end of June 2011. A friend immediately notified her that such pictures were circulating through "emails and message boards." When Duke looked into it, she realized that the pictures present were nude photographs she had sent as an undergrad at Clemson University, to her boyfriend when she was merely 18 years old. Duke, 24 at the time the pictures surfaced, was mortified. Within a consecutive couple of weeks, Duke was contacted by her employer, Sprint, who fired her over the phone. Even though Duke was not given the opportunity to explain the pictures, she understood the action because she violated a morality clause in her contract. She says, "I lost my job, the best job I could have asked for, it was perfect for me." Here, the aspects of social media were used negatively and ruined not only a young girls reputation and self-confidence, but more importantly her dream job.[1]

However, despite all of the negativity, Duke chose to rise above it. After a couple of weeks spent figuring everything out, she chose to aim for a path that would reveal to the public who she really was. Instead of running from her story, she planned to tell it. She said, "I know I'm a good person. I know I have a good heart. I have good morals, I do. And I know that was a lapse in judgment then but I can live with myself because I know what kind of person I am. So that's why it was easier to tell my story." Even though someone else used social media to negatively portray Duke, the aftermath consisted of social media being used as a way to rebuild herself and self-esteem.

Two support pages arose on Facebook. By telling her story, she sought to inform other young girls about the consequences of actions on social media and to teach those how to avoid situations like the one she was placed in. After this, she said, "a bunch of people on Twitter started saying, 'I shared your story with my 13-year-old daughter,' or 'I sent your story to my daughter in college.' 'Thank you for sharing your story. I know it took a lot of courage. But now I can use your story in hopes that my daughter will learn a lesson from you.'" Duke also has had numerous other opportunities arise from the responsibility she took from her actions as well as her efforts to restore her public image. Perhaps the most influential opportunity to arise is the fact that Duke landed herself as the star on CMT reality TV show, Sweet Home Alabma. Reflected back, she said "it was a life-changing experience – it gave me my confidence back with everything that happened with NASCAR, it gave me a chance to be myself and for me to be out in the public eye again for something good and for people to see really how I was." [2]

Social media does not only effect celebrity's lives in our world, it also happens at a more local level as well. Within each area there are personal stories which may not have been as publicized, but do and have had serious effects on the lives of those involved. To bring your attention to this concern, here are two personal stories, involving social media from completely different contexts, yet both are from a small town – New Martinsville, WV.

In January 2012, a brutal beating was filmed behind the New Martinsville Elementary School. The video consisted of the victim, Josh Scarborough, 19, being brutally beaten by his attacker, Johnathan Johnson, 20. Not only were these individuals involved wrong for filming such an event, they took it one step further and posted the video on the social media website, YouTube. After the victim was taken to Wetzel County Hospital, local police authorities began investigating. New Martinsville Police Department initiated the investigation, by finding the actual link to the YouTube video on Johnson's Facebook page. Not only did Johnson post this link, he also openly boasted on his page about his conquest. Because of this, authorities were able to make the arrest just two hours and 42 minutes from the start of their investigation. Johnson was charged with malicious wounding and is currently awaiting trial. However, the lurking question is who was filming? Although no others have been caught yet, the investigation is continuing further and if discovered, according to Prosecuting Attorney Timothy Haught, "if they can be charged, they will be charged." [3]

The third story portrays an entirely different aspect to consequences that can arise through personal postings on social media. A local young woman from New Martinsville, West Virginia shared her story about how her constant ignorant comments she posted on Facebook throughout high school affected her present as well as her future. This young woman posted embarrassing and instigative comments on Facebook to members of a rival cheerleading squad her senior year in high school because her squad had just successfully beat the other team in a competition. Ironically, however, she ended up getting to know, and eventually dated, one of the rival cheerleader's brothers. The comments she once posted, however, had already circulated the town of the rival team – Weirton, West Virginia – which is a fairly small, close-knit community. As the relationship between the two continued further, and deepened, the young woman had to go to various events and be seen by the community, who had heard of the things she had said. However, the comments posted did not show the true side of this girl. She set out to regain the town's trust and repair her reputation by just being her up-beat and very personable self. When I asked her what she learned from this experience she said, "I learned that although it may be easy to simply press a few keys and click post, that most things are better left unsaid. It has become inevitably obvious that the decisions of my past were a bit off base. I have since then withheld from posting potentially significant material online." [4]

Despite these stories that more or less portray how social media can be abused and used harmfully in people's lives, there are many cases out there that focus on the exact opposite. Many people are truly taking advantage of the opportunites that come with social media, whether it be spreading their message to millions across the web, or sharing personal, inspirational stories to those who are a bit hesitant of social media. The purpose of social media is to ultimately be used as a positive tool. So, keep in mind that regardless of the harms and personal experiences given above, there are many instances out there that reflect upon the positive. Our society today is prone to targeting and spreading nothing but the negative stories, which is why I want to expose you to a few ways that social media is being used to positively change and even save lives.

The first positive social media story comes from the Children's Miracle Network. On June 4, 2011, the Children's Miracle Network launched their new online campaign called 100 Million Miracles, which uses social media to spread their message. The goal of this program is to use social media to raise $100 million to help more than 17 million children and families that the organization supports each year. This campaign is not solely being carried out by the Children's Miracle Network, but also by its supports, including Delta Airlines, that are also using their social media channels to spread the word to support children's hospitals across North America. this campaign can also be spread by individuals just like you! The Children's Miracle Network has organized their campaign so that people all throughout the United States can use their own social media accounts to share the message and advertise the program by posting the website www.100millionmiracles.com on their profiles. Since 1983, Children's Miracle Network Hospitals have raised more than $4 billion, guarantying that every dollar goes to helping local children and saving as many lives as possible. [5]

Children's Miracle Network took using social media one step further with the creation of Hospitopia, an online social media game. After reviewing statistics from the Children's Miracle Network article—Facebook has 500 million active users each month, in comparison to about 300 million people living across the country—they decided it clearly made sense for them to be present on this World Wide Web phenomenon. Because of this, they decided to make their presence known of Facebook. Not only does the Children's Miracle Network have their own Facebook page to highlight fundraising events, tell you about campaigns, and spread information about what is going on within their hospital network, they also created the virtual game of Hospitopia.

Within this game, people get to build and manage their own virtual hospital and perform the tasks necessary to run it, including caring and treating children, "generating donations through fundraisers, purchasing medicine through Miracle Points, and earning experience points through the quality of care to raise the level of the hospital." In doing so, they actually get to help raise money for a local Children's Miracle Network hospital. The game's creator will donate ten percent of all the game's gross revenue to the Children's Miracle Network hospitals. Users even have the option to specify which hospital to benefit, earning the facility there special prizes and other incentives. Craig Sorenson, chief marketing officer for Children's Miracle Network Hospitals said, "With nearly 27 percent of the U.S. population paying social games, the time felt right...to expand fundraising tactics into this growing space." [6]

A second website that is using social media as a way to inspire people is Twitter. Twitter is not only a top social networking site, but it has also furthered its occupation on the web and branched a new website called Twitter Stories, which you can view by going to http://stories.twitter.com/. This website aims to allow viewers on the web to read about inspiring and life changing stories that have happened on social media, or more specifically by posting nothing more than a 140 character tweet on their Twitter page. A few of the stories that can be found on the page can be something so huge as to writing a book and landing a movie deal, or something so basic such as someone who used Twitter to save a dog's life. Here are some direct excerpts taken from the website to give you a general idea of what all you can discover and learn about:

"Myra McEntire wrote a book, found an agent, got published and landed a movie deal using Twitter every step of the way. She found critique partners to help her through the writing process and followed publishers and agents to learn what they wanted in new submissions. When her book was published her followers helped bump her title to the top of summer reading lists and gather the attention of Hollywood. She said, 'I figured out that Twitter was wildly different from other social media. It was a conversation, a real time relationship. I followed those agents whose blogs I used to haunt.'"

"When a stray dog collapsed in front of Mark Hayward's home, his first thought was to try to save her. A ferry ride to the nearest vet revealed that the dog suffered from malnutrition, dehydration, mange and a deeply entrenched heartworm parasite. The dog could be saved—the only problem was the cost. Mark tweeted a plea for help to his followers, but the response wasn't enough to pay for the dog's needs. Not ready to give up, he then tweeted to actress and activist @Alyssa_Milano, who donated and retweeted his call for help. Her followers retweeted the request and within 24-hours they raised over $1000 to pay for the dog's recovery. The dog, now named Lilly, has fully recovered and lives with an adopted family in Charleston, South Carolina, USA."

"Chris Strouth had been living with kidney disease for three years, but suddenly it was getting worse. He needed a transplant. Not knowing what else to do, he turned to Twitter and wrote: 'Sh*t, I need a kidney' Within a few days, 19 people offered to find out if they might be a match. One of the people who replied was an acquaintance named Scott Pakudaitis, who hadn't seen Chris in years. After seeing the Tweet, Scott researched the procedure, talked to people who had been through it before, then decided to get tested to see if he would be a match. When the match came back positive, he decided to donate his kidney. After the procedure, he sent a get-well-soon message to back to Strouth—on Twitter." [7]

These individual stories from the website truly amaze me has to how much people can do with a simple 140 character tweet. The website offers a great opportunity for the world to connect on social media through inspiring stories. Twitter Stories offers a unique experience that exasperates the positives and benefits social networking and social media websites can have on one, or even multiple lives. If you are ever bored, or curious about social media, I encourage you to check out this website – it's truly inspiring.

Reflecting back on this entire experience, I realized that there are many negatives to social media a person can get wrapped up in, which can potentially change or even ruin life as they know it. I hope that the personal stories I shared with you were helpful in realizing and identifying with this aspect. However, I feel that through including the many positive stories that are out there that you can see that so many people in our world are not taking social media for granted, but are in fact using it for not only their benefit, but for the benefit of others as well.

The most important notion I want you all to get from my chapter is, be careful. It is essential to be aware of the dangers and risks on the web; however, I encourage you to not be afraid of it, yet embrace it like so many in our world have done today and will continue doing in the future. Social media is not going anywhere, so why not try it out? However, whenever you do decide to log on for the first time, do not allow yourself to be swept up in the wonders of the web, but continue to be mindful with each and every post. Or, if it would help, follow Paige Duke's rule of thumb for social media: "Don't do anything you wouldn't want your grandma to see." [8]

REFERENCES

1. "Ex-Miss Sprint Cup Paige Duke Speaks Out About Nude Pics." *FoxCharlotte*, July 6, 2011. http://www.foxcharlotte.com/news/local/Ex-Miss-Sprint-Cup-Paige-Duke-Speaks-Out--125118929.html (accessed February 20, 2012).

2. Johnson, Kris. "Scene Daily." Last modified August 3, 2011. Accessed February 20, 2012. http://www.scenedaily.com/news/articles/sprintcupseries/Former_Miss_Sprint_Cup_PaigP_Duke_lands_new_job_feels_like_victim_after_nude_photos_surfaced.html.

3. "Beating Put on YouTube Results in Man's Arrest." *Wetzel Chronicle*, January 11, 2012. http://www.wetzelchronicle.com/page/content.detail/id/510569.html (accessed February 21, 2012).

4. Patterson, Emily. February 25, 2012.

5. McHugh, Kenna. Children's Miracle Network, "Social Times." Last modified June 3, 2011. Accessed February 20, 2012. http://socialtimes.com/childrens-miracle-network-uses-social-media-to-raise-100-million_b65077.

6. "The NonProfit Times." Last modified February 8, 2012. Accessed February 20, 2012. http://www.thenonprofittimes.com/article/detail/childrens-miracle-network-launches-social-game-1506.

7. Twitter, "Twitter Stories." Accessed February 21, 2012. http://stories.twitter.com/.

8. "Ex-Miss Sprint Cup Paige Duke Speaks Out About Nude Pics." *FoxCharlotte*, July 6, 2011. http://www.foxcharlotte.com/news/local/Ex-Miss-Sprint-Cup-Paige-Duke-Speaks-Out--125118929.html (accessed February 20, 2012).

CHAPTER 15

Grace Williams – "When It's Gone, is it Really Gone?"

1. Who has access to an account after ones passing?

2. Are accounts deleted once someone passes?

3. How does one tell Facebook that the user has passed?

What happens to deleted pics, posts, and entire accounts? What about deleting friends?

So it's Sunday morning, err... afternoon. You already know what the stereotypical college kid did last night. The same thing you did on Saturday nights when you were our age, and if you don't know, use your imagination. The only difference is, these days, the entire world could potentially know exactly what we did, who we were with, and where we were within minutes.

If you went to college in the '60's, '70's, '80's, or even the '90's you were lucky. You didn't have to worry about that. If there was any documentation of wild parties or stupid dares, chances are it was in the form of an old-fashioned camera with actual film that had to be taken to the drug store and developed, a process that usually took a few days or at least hours, or the evidence was scribbled in your college girlfriends' old diaries. In either case, those memories were just that, memories. Sure, the stories could spread by word of mouth, and eventually the whole campus could kind of know what happened, but still it would be their word against yours. Except in the unlikely event that copies were made of those embarrassing pictures, there was no definite proof, and if there was, the pictures could be burned, shredded, or destroyed. Today, we live in a different age, a digital age.

Today, a photograph can be taken with a cell phone and a Facebook comment can be typed in mere second. Now, depending on a Facebook user's privacy setings, hundreds, thousands, or potentially millions of people can view that embarassing posted material instantly. Deleting it's not a problem. Right? Well, it's actually not that simple.

According to *My Fox Boston*, photos that are deleted on Facebook can last months or even years on Facebook servers, however viewing them requires a very specific URL. They're still out there, but not immediately accessible unless you have that URL saved. In other words, if your room-mate uploads a photo and tags you in it, before you get the chance to delete it, your ex-boyfriend can copy and paste the link; then he can pull that photo up anytime he wants until Facebook purges its servers. The worst thing is, there is nothing you can do about it. [1]

Maybe this situation is kind of dramatic. Maybe you're thinking that people who choose to put themselves in situations that are embarrass-ing if captured by camera deserve to be humiliated. Point taken. But let's take this into consideration. We have all looked back at a photo of ourselves at some point and thought it was either embarrassing or unflat-tering. Those would be nice to delete too if we wanted.

Here's a personal story. I am a junior in college, and I've had a Facebook since I was a junior in high school. That's four years of my life that I have voluntarily documented online. Weird, right? But it's not only weird, it can be scary too. Sometimes I go through all my old tagged pictures just for the heck of it and feel like I'm watching a slide show of my life. Looking through the close to one thousand photos of myself and the thirty albums I have posted is both enthralling and creepy. Well, at least I have my Facebook on its maximum privacy settings so only my friends can see my photos. But wait, my Facebook friend count is currently at 671! Do all 671 of those "friends" really deserve to know that much about me?

Why do I have that many friends anyway? Is it really necessary for me to stay in some kind of pseudo-contact with everyone I meet? I don't even consider Facebook real contact. Honestly, I talk to maybe 50 people on Facebook, ever. That kid from summer camp four years ago who I didn't even talk to when I was at camp and certainly have not made one single post or comment to since adding him as a friend on Facebook – keep him or delete him?

This leads me to my next point about deleting friends. Is there some kind of unwritten law saying that if you delete someone, you hate them? Will they even notice that we aren't "friends" anymore? A Facebook relationship between "friends" should not be compared to a real life friendship. If I delete someone, it doesn't mean we got in a fight and I don't like them anymore. Rather, it means it just isn't worth it to be online friends. We don't talk, and quite frankly, I just don't care anymore. Sorry. That does sound kind of mean.

After friends are deleted they can no longer view your private Facebook page or your photos. Deleted friends do not receive a notice of deletion, and chances are they won't even notice that you aren't friends anymore. The online "relationship" will simply be the same as it was before you two friended each other to begin with.

Not only is Facebook a source of much stress and angst for its young users, it is also a major distraction, and sometimes even a little bit scary. I sit down at my desk to work on a specific project, open my laptop, and pull up Microsoft Word to work on a paper. Before I know it, I have been on Facebook for forty-five minutes and I don't even know why! Even since I've been writing this very chapter, I'm sure I have spent close to an hour on Facebook. The window just seems to open, and then I'm logged in, looking at my newsfeed, Facebook stalking a friend of a friend of a friend.

We have established that Facebook can be distracting and stressful sometimes, but it can also be a little frightening at times. For instance, Facebook can actually recognize a face! If that's not creepy, then I don't know what is! Here's how it works. According to Sarah Jacobsson Purewal on PC World, Facebook is "gathering data and recognizing your face."[2]

For the past several years, Facebook has encouraged its users to tag photos. That seems harmless, right? So of course we all started tagging our photos by placing the curser directly over the image of someone's face, scrolling through a friend list, and selecting the name that matches the face. We've all been doing this for years now.

Now when a photo is uploaded to Facebook, a window opens that not only prompts the user to tag the people in the photo, but also suggests who that person may be. Strange, but here is how it works. There are enough files saved in Facebook cyberspace with our names attached to them. The images may all be slightly different, but close enough to be identified as our faces. It's as though the computers have face recognition. And they are pretty accurate! But one time, Facebook did try to tag me as my sister. I guess we do look a lot alike.

'Till Death Do Us Part; What Happens When We Die

In a day and age when everyone is online, plugged in, blogging, posting, pinning, liking, tweeting, and retweeting, "What about the ones that died?" you may ask.

"Yep, they're online, too!" college students might say nonchalantly, while simultaneously checking our Twitter on our iPads, texting our roommates on our cell phones, and talking to our friends about plans to Facebook stalk that girl from high school who just got married, and OMG did you see her bridesmaids' dresses and is she seriously naming her baby that?!

"Hold on! What?" you're thinking. "How on earth can someone who has passed away still have an active account on the internet?"

Well, this isn't exactly earth, my friend. It's cyberspace! That's right. Apparently when God takes people from our presence, He doesn't automatically take their Facebook, MySpace, Pinterest, Twitter, Paypal, Linkedin, Flickr, Amazon, Ebay, or even email accounts with them to heaven. I can't quite decide if that's good or bad, but it certainly seems strange.

These days, so many people lead a sort of "double life." We post our entire personalities and every life event on social networking sites such as Facebook. It's almost as if we are marrying our online accounts, "till death do us part." As we all know by now, social networking has its pros and cons. Let's take a closer look at some pros and cons of accounts remaining after a loved one has passed.

Some people say keeping friends or family members' Facebook accounts active after they have passed away is a great way to get closure, say goodbye, keep online conversations, and reminisce by browsing through old photos and posts. On the other hand, trying to deal with privacy, finding out unknown passwords, and deciding who, if anyone, gets access to the accounts can be a headache and cause more unnecessary frustration and heartache following the death of a loved one.

Time Magazine Online suggests that a solution to this confusion and stress is to memorialize the Facebook page. By memorializing a Facebook page, the deceased person's page is removed from public search. The account is then sealed from any future log-in attempts. The person stops showing up in friends' news feeds, and his or her name no longer shows up in the suggested friend list. The wall and inbox still remain open for Facebook friends to leave posts, comments, and messages. In order for a Facebook account to be memorialized, proof of death such as an obituary is required to deter pranks. If a family prefers not to keep the Facebook of a deceased person as a memorial, it can also be removed and permanently deleted.[3]

The State, one of South Carolina's online newspapers, suggests another option to prevent causing the loved ones we leave behind so much pain. *The State* suggests that we include our "digital assets" in our will, or at least write down our accounts, usernames, and passwords and keep them in a safe place so that someone we trust can have access to or delete the accounts when we die. Digital accounts are not as tangible as physical possessions and often do not seem as immediate; therefore they often get overlooked. [4]

After hearing the story of a young Marine killed in Iraq whose parents had to go to court in order to acquire their son's Yahoo email account, two young entrepreneurs in Madison, Wisconsin co-founded Entrustet in 2008, which is a business that allows clients to appoint a "digital executer" who will inherit access to all of their online accounts after they die. According to *The State*, a handful of other businesses with the same goal have formed in the past few years, allowing the "digital executer" to have permission to delete, keep active, or transfer whichever accounts the deceased client wished.

I hope that as I leave you with these few words of wisdom, you are not frightened of Facebooking, leery of Linking In, or terrified of Tweeting. Rather, I hope that you are able to take this information and proceed with your normal social media activities, and maybe even broaden your horizons but doing so as a much more cautious and informed user.

Remember, even though it may seem as though we marry our online accounts, and yeah they do remain after we die, and yeah it is difficult to delete certain things, maybe, just maybe it's worth it.

"Are Your Facebook Photos Really Deleted?" *MyFox Boston.* Myfoxboston.com, 7 Feb. 2012. Web. 26 Mar. 2012. <http://www.myfoxboston.com/dpps/news/technology/are-your-facebook-photos-really-deleted-dpgoh-20120207-fc_17721730>.

Purewal, Sarah J. "Why Facebook's Facial Recognition Is Creepy." *PCWorld.* Pcworld.com, 8 June 2011. Web. 27 Mar. 2012. <http://www.pcworld.com/article/229742/why_ facebooks_facial_ recognition_ is_creepy.html>.

Fletcher, Dan. "What Happens to Your Facebook After You Die?" *Time.* Time, 28 Oct. 2009. Web. 26 Mar. 2012. <http://www.time.com/time/business/article/0,8599,1932803,00.html>.

1. "What Happens to Facebook Page When You Die?" *Thestate.com.* The State; South Carolina's Homepage, 25 Dec. 2011. Web. 26 Mar. 2012. <http://www.thestate.com/2011/12/25/2091213/what-happens-to-facebook-page.html>.

Quizes brought to you by Patrick Callahan.

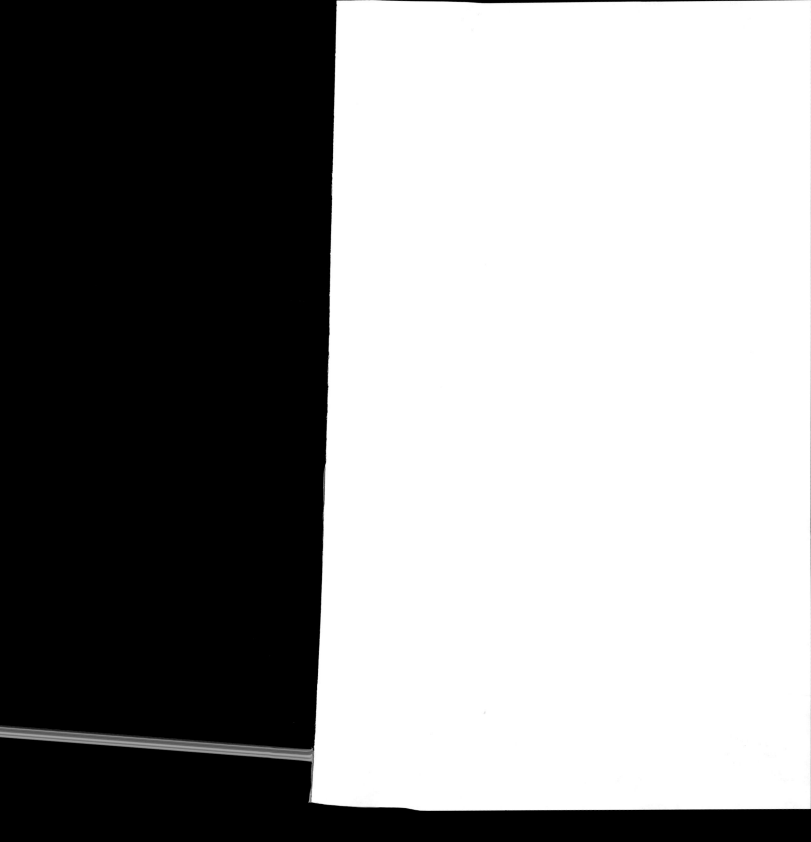